The World of Crime

Mark Llewellin & Peter Riley
Foreword by Edward Woodward OBE

P & D Riley

First published 2004

P & D Riley
12 Bridgeway East,
Cheshire,
WA7 6LD,
England

E-mail: pdriley@ntlworld.com

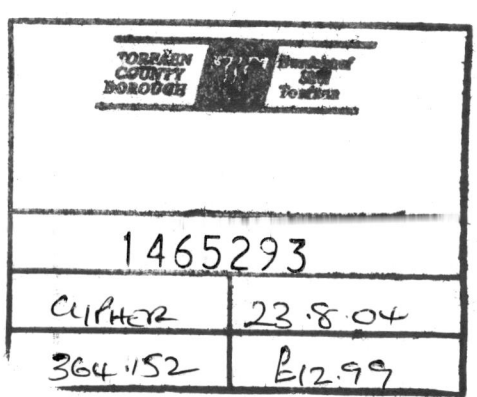

Copyright © 2004 by Mark Llewellin and Peter Riley
Foreword © 2004 by Edward Woodward OBE

ISBN: 1 874712 67 0 (Hardback)
ISBN: 1 874712 74 3 (Paperback)

British Library Cataloguing in Publication Data
A catalogue Record for this book is available from the British Library

All rights reserved. No part of this publication may be reproduced, stored in a retrieval system, or transmitted, in any form or by any means, electronic, mechanical, photocopying, recording or otherwise, without the permission of the publisher and the copyright owner.

Printed by CPI Bath

About the authors

Mark Llewellin trained in performing arts at Wakefield College. He has had a varied career including a stint as a guide at London's Highgate Cemetery, several years with London Transport and seven years as Marketing Director at Oldham Coliseum Theatre. These days he is a director of the marketing consultancy Volcano Associates and a freelance writer.

Mark is a seasoned performer on stage and radio and is much in demand as a guest/expert. Most recently he has appeared on 'Inside Out', 'North West Tonight' and 'This is Your Life' for the BBC and 'Mystery Hunters' for Discovery (Canada). He can be regularly heard on local radio and had his own weekly BBC GMR slot for over a year. His first book *They Started Here!* was published in 2000.

Peter Riley is a professional writer, journalist and publisher who has worked for numerous newspapers and magazines in Britain, contributing articles on local history, topography and true crime. He has also written and appeared in more than 100 radio programmes, several of them covering true crime subjects featured in this book. He also wrote and presented a BBC radio series on Victorian detective Jerome Caminada of Manchester, and wrote and co-produced a local history quiz for the BBC. His TV appearances include BBC TV's 'Tonight' programme and 'Look North West', and ITV's 'Frost on Sunday' and 'Crown Court'.

He is also the author of *The Highways and Byways of Jack the Ripper* and *An Illustrated Guide to Jack the Ripper* as well as numerous local history books.

Acknowledgements

The authors and publishers would like to thank the following
for their help in the preparation of this book

Edward Woodward OBE for kindly writing the Foreword
Clifford and Marie Elmer of Clifford Elmer Books, Cheadle Hulme,
England, for permission to use their modern photographs
of Fall River and the Lizzie Borden house
Fall River Herald News for allowing us to reproduce the
pictures taken inside the Borden house.
Loretta Lay of Loretta Lay Books, London
Ms. Ping Liu, Reference Librarian, Round Rock Public Library, Texas
Jean James of British Columbia, Canada
Pat Devlin, The Book Loft, Warrington, Cheshire, England
Volcano Associates
Joel Chester Fildes

Authors' Note: Inevitably, when writing about real cases, one relies heavily on accounts published at the time. We are therefore indebted to the many authors and photographers who went before us.

Foreword by Edward Woodward OBE

When I was a boy I would sit with my mother and father in the kitchen every evening, cosied up in front of the coal fired range, listening to the wireless. Once a month we would go to the picture house and sink into a glorious fantasy world of beautiful women and handsome men living in their luxurious houses or grand apartments, in a land where the sun always shone in the summer and the snow covered them in the winter, and they never seemed to stop dancing and singing indoors or outdoors whatever the weather! (somewhat different to living in a two-up and two-down in Broadway Avenue, Croydon, Surrey!)

My main source of entertainment, however, was reading. I read everything I could lay hands on, especially books on crime. In my day the most popular books borrowed from public libraries were accounts of major crimes and the ensuing trials. I also devoured the daily papers. The newspapers of the nineteen-thirties carried on the 19th century tradition of giving verbatim reports of all serious crimes, especially the heinous crime of murder, and the great lawyers of the time, men like Edward Marshall Hall and Patrick Hastings, were treated like filmstars. The reading public lapped up every nuance, every twist and turn of a clever defence or a brilliant prosecution, and we were pulled into a world of horror and excitement – a world where good nearly always triumphed over evil.

When Messrs Llewellin and Riley sent me the final draft of this book and asked me to write these few words, I plunged into 'The World of Crime' with great interest and anticipation. I was not disappointed – I know you will feel the same. Each account captures the very essence of the crime reported, from the chilling evil of Charlie Peace in the mid 19th century to Victor Lustig who flourished as the greatest 'con-man' in the 1930s. We are taken on a fascinating and exciting journey through the lives of both criminal and victim.

This is a book you can dip into, however I'm sure that, like me, once you've started you won't want to put it down. My only regret is that it isn't long enough!

So welcome to a great read. I can't wait to read the next one.

My good wishes to you all

Edward Woodward OBE

Few British performers can come close to Edward Woodward for variety in their show business career. Born in Surrey in 1930 he made his first stage appearance in 1946 and his film debut in *Where There's a Will* in 1955. In 1967 he was cast as David Callan in the TV Armchair Theatre play *A Magnum for Schneider* in which he made such an impact that the show became the TV series *Callan* that ran for five years.

Although *Callan* gave him a worldwide following, Edward appeared in many light entertainment shows, ranging from *The Morecambe and Wise Show* to *The Good Old Days*, where his superb voice entertained a whole new group of fans. He also appeared in many classic TV series such as *The Saint* and *Young Winston*, and has appeared twice as the subject of the long-running programme *This is Your Life*.

Although appearing in many films and other television shows, it was the crime show *The Equalizer*, an American production, that gave him worldwide fame once again when it was screened between 1985-89. Not content to be typecast, Edward hosted, between 1991 and 1995, the TV series *In Suspicious Circumstances* that gave fascinating insights into many true crime tales.

Awarded an OBE in 1980, he now lives in London with his actress wife Michele.

THE ROAR OF THE GREASEPAINT ... THE SMELL OF MYSTERY!
Two tales from London's West End

PERHAPS the best-known theatrical murder took place at the stage door of the Adelphi Theatre in London's busy West End.

The Adelphi was originally opened as the 'Sans Pareil' back in 1806 but was re-named when it changed hands in 1819. By the mid-nineteenth century the theatre had established itself as the home of melodrama, indeed George Bernard Shaw chronicled, "A really good Adelphi melodrama is of first rate literary importance because it only needs elaboration to become a masterpiece." One actor became more publically associated with this form of entertainment than any other - William Terriss, a remarkably handsome and debonair actor. Terriss was born in North London in 1847, the son of a barrister, he entered the navy at the tender age of fourteen and subsequently tried his hand at engineering and tea planting before deciding that the stage was his true calling. He had a glittering career working on many productions with the great Henry Irving, subsequently the first theatrical knight, at the Lyceum before joining the Adelphi company in 1879.

London theatregoers took the young actor, he was just thirty-two, to their hearts and a true star was born. Off the stage he was happily married and his life was a settled one - he also became a bit of a hero when he rescued a drowning family from the sea whilst visiting Kent. So on and off stage, he was the dashing and gallant romantic pin-up. On December 16th 1897 Terriss arrived at the Adelphi's stage door to make for his dressing room in preparation for another full house for the hit play 'Secret Service' but it was sadly to be his closing night. From out of the shadows jumped out-of-work and somewhat deranged actor Richard Prince who set about Terriss with a knife, fatally injuring him.

The historian Lynton Hudson wrote, "His murder marked the passing of the kind of melodrama so long associated with the theatre where he died." Terriss' funeral was attended by thousands of wailing devoted fans and the Daily Telegraph launched an appeal to name a lifeboat after him - indeed, such was the amount of cash raised that a whole lifeboat house was built in his honour at Eastbourne. In 1997, exactly a century after his tragic demise, Sir Donald Sinden unveiled a plaque at the Adelphi marking the murder of this immensely popular actor. He was survived by his daughter, Ellaline, who became a celebrated actress in her own right and married Seymour Hicks, another famous theatrical impressario.

The Adelphi as it looks today

What is often ignored by historians is the link between the unfortunate Terriss and Prince. In fact, Prince had been employed by the great actor, albeit in minor roles, but due to his drinking and unreliability had been fired. Terriss however had shown himself to be an honourable man and had personally recommended Prince to the Actors Benevolent Fund for a hand out.

The World of Crime

Top: A plaque in memory of William Terriss

Middle: The stage door of the Adelphi Theatre

Bottom: Henry Irving as Shylock. This great actor regularly worked with the young Terriss

The World of Crime

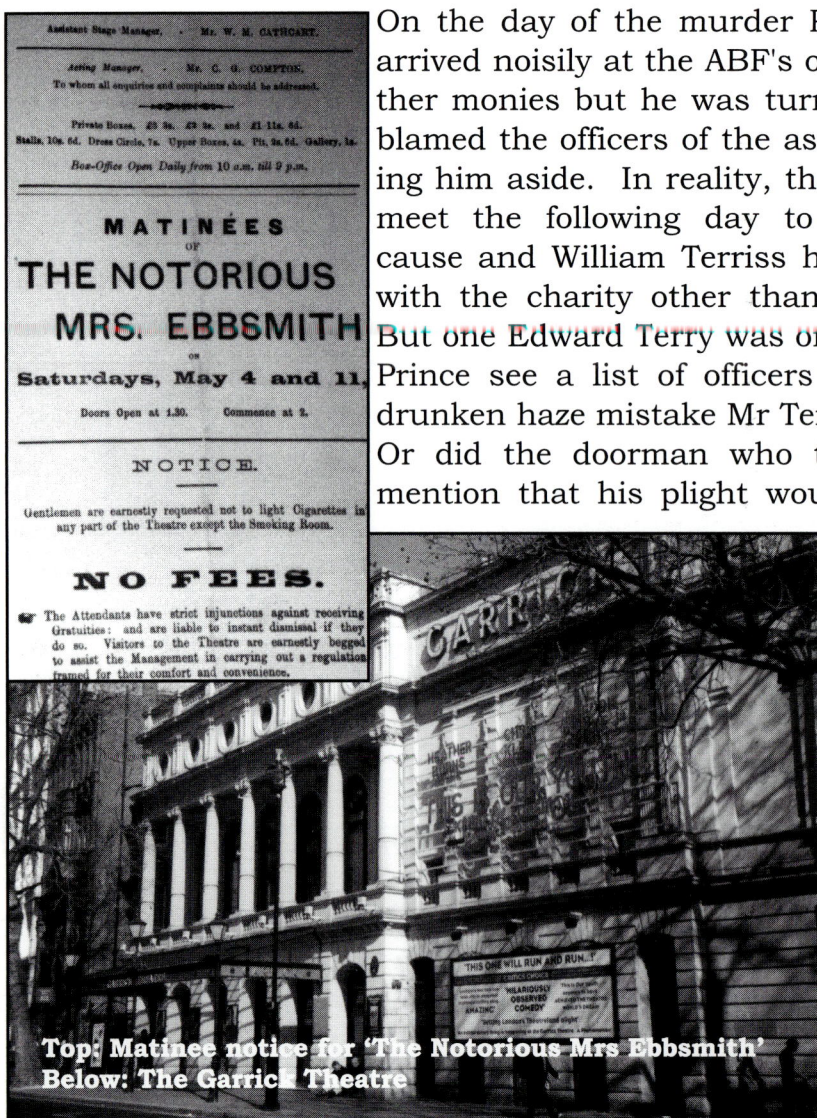

Top: Matinee notice for 'The Notorious Mrs Ebbsmith'
Below: The Garrick Theatre

On the day of the murder Prince had indeed arrived noisily at the ABF's offices seeking further monies but he was turned away - Prince blamed the officers of the association for casting him aside. In reality, the trustees were to meet the following day to discuss Prince's cause and William Terriss had no connection with the charity other than through friends. But one Edward Terry was on the council - did Prince see a list of officers and through his drunken haze mistake Mr Terry for Mr Terriss? Or did the doorman who turned him away mention that his plight would be brought to Mr Terry's attention thus confusing him further? Did Prince cross the street to Maiden Lane looking to show Mr Terry a thing or two? - was in fact, the wrong man killed?

Another curious little mystery concerns the Garrick Theatre. In the spring of 1895, the theatre staged a production of Arthur Wing Pinero's drama 'The Notorious Mrs Ebbsmith' starring amongst others Gerald Du Maurier, Mrs Patrick Campbell and the theatre's director John Hare. During the run the body of a woman was found floating face down in the cold murky waters of the Thames. The police quickly established that she had drowned - probably committed suicide. Her name was Mrs Ebbsmith and she had in her coat pocket a ticket for the production. It later transpired that she had told a friend of seeing the play and that it's title had preyed on her mind - to such an extent, it would seem, that she had decided to end it all. Just why remains a mystery and the tale, a curiosity of Victorian theatre life.

THE CAD AND THE BRIGHT YOUNG THING!
The mysterious death of Michael Scott Stephen

FOLLOWING the Great War came a heady period of exuberance and frivolity - people were genuinely glad to be alive and those with money flaunted their freedom and excess. In the 1920's debutantes, balls, jazz, drink and a certain amount of promiscuity threatened to engulf the new young set.

Amongst those making a name for herself on the London social circuit was the twenty-seven-year-old daughter of Sir John and Lady Mullens, Elvira Barney. Armed with a parental allowance and a settlement following a brief marriage, Elvira, young, arrogant and brash, threw herself with some gusto onto the 'scene'. She found the ideal partner - Michael Scott Stephen, a failed dress designer, gambler and using the period talk, a 'cad'. It didn't stop them setting up home together though, at a luxury mews in Knightsbridge, with Elvira footing all the bills. Here they partied, quarrelled and lead something of a scandalous lifestyle, which eventually resulted in disaster. At around midnight on 31st May 1932 Elvira's doctor received a panicked phone call - his patient urged him to call at the house, which he agreed to do. Lying on the bedroom floor was the body of Michael Stephen, a fatal bullet from a .32 Smith and Wesson revolver punctured his chest. The gun lay by his feet, both chambers were empty.

As the doctor pronounced him dead, Elvira Barney cried out that she should be allowed to kill herself - she wanted to die with him. Soon the police were on the scene and Elvira was asked to accompany them to the local police station. She struck out and hit the unfortunate constable before being allowed to telephone her parents. "Now you know who my mother is, you will be more careful of what you say!" she shouted. It didn't stop her being hauled off for questioning and she explained the events of the night. The pair had, she said, returned home from a drinking session at the Café de Paris in a somewhat inebriated state. Stephen had announced his intention to leave her and she had in return threatened to kill herself. She produced the revolver, which she had kept hidden behind a cushion, he leapt at her in an attempt to snatch the gun from her and a struggle ensued. The gun went off - and Stephen lay dead.

Elvira Barney was released while the police went about their investigations but three days later she was formally arrested. The police were convinced by the testimony of neighbours - one had witnessed her threatening Stephen with a revolver in the mews, one heard her refuse him money and warn him it was the last time and one reported increasingly violent rows. It was powerful stuff and Elvira found herself on trial at the Old Bailey.

There was much technical evidence against her - the bullet had not been fired at close range in fact, the angle of the bullet suggested it had been shot from some distance. A gunsmith surmised that the weight of the trigger precluded it from having been fired accidentally, and, two shots had been fired - one hitting the wall. What kind of accident was it that happened twice?

In her defence, Sir Patrick Hastings claimed Elvira had suicidal tendencies and anyone over-hearing her threatening to shoot herself could have interpreted it as being a threat against her lover's life. It was also suggested that the bullet in the wall remained from an earlier innocent accident. Hastings had one more trick up his sleeve - he brandished the gun and fired it towards the court ceiling demonstrating how easy it was for a man to fool around with - an accident was possible. Elvira's own testimony was as a heartbroken lover, Hastings' summing up was compelling. The jury found her not guilty after just two hours deliberations.

Elvira Barney decided that she wanted to start a new life and she emigrated to France. At the same time, Sir Patrick Hastings decided to take his family to the continent on a well-earned holiday and so it turned out that the two leading players in the case arrived in Boulogne at the same time. It was here that Hastings narrowly escaped death in a motor accident when his car was hit by another vehicle driving at speed - behind the wheel, Elvira Barney. Another uninvestigated but curious twist to this sorry saga!

Just four years later and she was dead having committed suicide in her Paris apartment. She was just thirty-one. The bright young thing was extinguished.

The body of Michael Scott Stephen being removed from the Mews

THE SIEGE OF SIDNEY STREET
How a robbery went down in history

THE New Year had hardly begun and the people of London's East End were barely recovered from their celebrations of the start of 1911, when the cheery cockneys were treated to a spectacle that would be a talking point for many a long day. For on January 3rd a siege occurred in Sidney Street, Whitechapel, which was to end in a conflagration, death and controversy.

The siege was itself a sequel to a series of events that had shocked London in the previous month when, on Friday, December 16th, 1910, three police officers, Constable Walter Choat, and Sergeants Robert Bentley and 'Daddy' Tucker, had been murdered and two others badly wounded in Houndsditch, after armed robbers had been disturbed in a burglary attempt at a jewellers shop in Exchange Buildings, Cutler Street.

Peter the Painter

Angry police were firm in their resolve to capture the killers, and an investigation by detectives soon led to the finger of suspicion pointing at Russian anarchists, and in particular at a group led by a man named as Peter Piaktow, nicknamed 'Peter the Painter' on account of his earning his living as a painter of street doors in France and Russia.

Further investigations led police to 100 Sidney Street, a four-storey house built of red brick in 1900. As police were aware that the house was in the middle of a densely populated area, it was decided to wait until most of the street's residents had gone to bed – not an easy thing to do in Whitechapel which kept late hours – before taking any action. This meant police had to endure waiting on what was a freezing night, with gusts of rain and sleet for company, but this bad weather was an asset in that it helped keep people off the normally packed streets.

Detective Inspector Frederick Wensley, one of the men leading the hunt for the killers, later wrote: "As time wore on, the prospects of the men attempting to steal out and so running into our hands grew fainter. Right up to this hour, it must be understood, we had only the foggiest notion of who was in the house besides the assassins -- if indeed they were there."

During the course of the night it was decided to evacuate all the residents in and around number 100, and more police arrived, many armed with antiquated weapons, including shotguns, old-fashioned bulldog revolvers, and even rifles borrowed from a shooting gallery! At about 3.30am the evacuation of 100 Sidney Street began with police rousing tenants of the house that was divided into rented rooms, and from this

**Top: Artillery in Sidney Street
Right: Home Secretary Winston Churchill watches the action with police officers**

Above: Troops prepare for action as police hold back the crowd in Sidney Street

found that one of the rooms was occupied by their suspects. Having persuaded the tenants to leave the building, police mulled over their next move but backed away from a proposal to rush the room as the stairs were so narrow and armed men in the bedroom could kill too many police before they were overpowered or killed themselves.

Wensley added: "All hope of getting at the men unawares had now been abandoned...and they could scarcely have failed to be aware of the stir in the lower part of the house. More police were sent for, to keep a wider area of streets clear, and we waited for day to break."

The decision to wait until daylight crept over London allowed crowds of East Enders, always glad of a free show, to gather in the streets. At around 7.20am Inspector Wensley and his team gathered in a nearby alley and one of the officers threw a stone at the windows of the room occupied by the suspects with the intention of ordering them to give themselves up. The response was not at all what the British officers expected, for the occupants, by now identified as suspected anarchists, opened up a volley of shots and one of the police officers, Detective Sergeant Benjamin Leeson, was hit in the chest. The next 30 minutes saw police cowering behind walls, pinned down by the heavy fire of German made automatic pistols. The antiquated weapons of the police were no match for the German guns and a request went out to send a detachment of Scots Guards based at the nearby Tower of London.

Home Secretary Winston Churchill authorised the use of troops and decided to visit the scene personally in company with senior police officers. Eighteen Scots Guards arrived on the scene carrying Lee Enfield rifles, the standard army weapon, and they took up positions with armed police, effectively hemming in the occupants at 100 Sidney Street.

Wensley described the scene. "Soldiers and police kept up an unremitting fire which was vigorously returned from the windows of the besieged house. Very early every pane of glass had been shattered, and the broken fragments littered the sidewalks. The men within fired from behind the fluttering curtains, and it was hard to detect their movements. A burst of firing would come first from one floor and then from another...various devices, including the exhibition of dummies in police uniform, were tried to induce the cornered men to expose themselves, but they never did."

By one-o-clock in the afternoon a whiff of smoke showed from an upper window and it was soon apparent that the house was on fire and troops and police readied themselves for a possible last effort dash from the house, but again they were disappointed. Instead the smoke grew thicker, but occasional shots still came from inside the building stopping firemen from dousing

Killed: Sgt Robert Bentley

Killed: PC Walter Choat

Killed: Sgt 'Daddy' Tucker

The World of Crime

Top Left: Sidney Street had become a slum by the 1930s

Top Right: Sir William Nott Bowers was Commissioner of the City of London Police at the time of the siege

Bottom: 100 Sidney Street pictured after the siege

the flames. The fire started on an upper floor, and by 2pm the house was a mass of flames and shooting had stopped.

Wensley added: "In the debris two charred bodies were found. One of them had been shot through the head, and the other had apparently died of suffocation. At the subsequent inquest a verdict of Justifiable Homicide was returned."

The bodies recovered from the inferno were identified as Fritz Svaars, a Latvian locksmith in his early twenties and a committed anarchist who had been convicted for robbery in his native country and had also been involved in a bank robbery in the USA, and William Sokoloff, nicknamed Joseph, a Russian watchmaker who had arrived in Britain ten years earlier and who had been suspected of being involved in several robberies at places where he had worked.

Detectives continued their inquiries, but no trace was found of Peter 'the Painter' Piatkow, despite a £500 reward offered by City of London police. By February, five men and three women were in custody on conspiracy charges, but two men and two women were released during committal proceedings.

The site of Exchange Buildings, Cutler Street, as it looks today

The three remaining men were committed to the Old Bailey for trial but were acquitted, leaving a sole woman prisoner to be convicted of conspiracy to burgle. She was sentenced to two years in prison, but this conviction was overturned on appeal, the appeal judges deciding that the trial jury had been misdirected. This left police frustrated, for nobody else was ever charged with the crimes, though they did gain consolation from the official line that the police killers were themselves dead, victims of the siege of Sidney Street.

Before Crippen

CRIMINOLOGISTS have often rightly proclaimed that wife-killer Doctor Harvey Hawley Crippen was the first man in the world to be captured thanks to the use of the newly invented radio, back in 1910.

But many would be surprised to learn that 80 years earlier, another killer named John Tawell was also captured and subsequently executed, thanks to another modern invention of the time – the electric telegraph!

On January 1st, 1845, a woman was murdered at Salt Hill, near Slough in Berkshire, and Tawell, a Quaker, with whom she had been intimate, was suspected of the crime. Tawell left the scene of the murder and made his way to Slough where he caught a train to London, certain that he had made his getaway courtesy of the newly invented railway.

However, astute police officers made use of the even more modern telegraph system and Tawell's description was wired to Paddington Station. When the suspect left the railway station he had no idea that he was being followed, and after a short period of observation police decided to move in and arrest him.

Tawell was tried, found guilty and subsequently executed for the murder.

A well known writer of the period, Sir Francis Head, recorded that while he was travelling on the same railway after the murder, he heard a third-class passenger, while pointing at the overhead telegraph wires, comment: "Them's the cords that hanged John Tawell!"

THE CINNAMON DRESS
The murder of Jess McPherson

GLASGOW in the 1860s - very much a city of two parts - rich and poor. Whilst the port and ship building families prospered, the poorer underclass fell deeper into poverty, debt and despair. Such was the setting for one of Scotland's most celebrated nineteenth century crimes.

Jess McLachlan was a twenty-eight-year-old frail, pretty and highly popular young wife. She lived with her sailor husband James in a tenement at Broomielaw Street in quite some state of poverty. Jess had suffered from heart problems since the birth of their child and with James away at sea for long periods, they relied heavily on the assistance of neighbours. In an attempt to make ends meet Jess let out various parts of her home to other sailors which meant that she often had nowhere to sleep but the floor of her own kitchen.

Jess had a number of friends dotted around the city - including another Jess - Jess McPherson, a thirty-eight-year-old servant who worked for a wealthy family, the Flemings. The Flemings were well known locally and ran a family accountancy business in the city. At their home, in Sandyford Place, resided the grandfather, one Mr Fleming senior, who had something of a reputation as a drunk and a lecher. Old Mr Fleming was known to have tried it on with both the young women and even called at Jess McPherson's tenement apartment on several occasions.

Such was the backdrop to the case. On the night of the murder, Friday July 4th 1862, Jess McLachlan had arranged to visit her friend at Sandyford Place. The Flemings were away at their summer home in Dunoon but old Mr Fleming had been left at home. Jess McLachlan was deep in debt at the time, she had pawned much of her clothing and indeed, on this particular day asked a neighbour to collect her cloak from the local pawnbroker so she could go visiting in the evening - this was duly done for her. Jess dressed to go out - a light brown velvet bonnet, the light grey cloak over a fine wool brown dress - as she admired herself in the mirror, her young son was fast asleep. There then arrived unexpected visitors who had to be let in by a Mrs Campbell who lived nearest the street door - all visitors seemed to be admitted in this way.

Having explained that she was visiting a number of friends that night, including Jess at Sandyford Place, she left with her visitors, walking with them up Washington Street for about ten minutes. At just after ten o'clock she bid them farewell and headed off into the night. She had talked of calling at friends whose young child was ill on her way to Jess' but for whatever reason, she didn't do as she had discussed.

Twenty-eight town houses made up the crescent of Sandyford Place, just above Sauchiehall Street. Number seventeen was one of the few houses without a front garden, just a paved driveway fronting the pavement. Eight people resided there, including Jess who had a tiny room in the basement. At around ten PC Campbell strolled along the road on his Friday night beat, he would be back an hour later. At eleven the local liquor shop owner Mr Littlejohn shut up shop and climbed the stairs to retire for the night. A group of women stood gossiping on the street corner from where they saw a frail woman heading down the lane behind Sandyford Place, a man was seen nearby and they drew the conclusion that it must have been a prostitute and client.

Just after eleven PC Campbell passed by again. At around the same time a Mr Stewart, whose house stood next to number seventeen heard a scream through the wall. He listened for a while but heard no more. He fell back into his slumbers and all remained quiet in Sandyford Place until 3.40am when three residents, three sisters, returned home from a wedding celebration. One sister remarked how curious it was to see a light still burning in number seventeen's window. At six PC Campbell clocked off and PC Cameron took over the beat. At seven thirty the milkboy, a thirteen-year-old called Donald McQuarrie, came a calling and was taken aback to have old Mr Fleming answer the door rather than the servant girl.

Back at Broomielaw, the returning Jess McLachlan disturbed Mrs Campbell - it was 9am. Jess was dressed as she had left but she carried a bundle of clothes under her arm. She wasn't home for long - she left on the pretext of buying kindling wood but in fact, she had a busy couple of hours. She had a number of transactions to undertake at the pawnbrokers, she called at the ironmongers for several items including a hat-box, she paid off some debts with some silver items which were all stamped with 'F' and she paid the rent.

Meanwhile, back at number seventeen, there was an interesting development also. Jess often 'sub-contracted' some of her chores to a girl called Mary Brown. Mary had turned up for work as usual but had been asked by old Mr Fleming to carry out an unusual task - to clean a dark stain off the lobby floor. Mary was paid and left. Later in the day a friend of Jess' came to see her but he was told she wasn't at home and he left. On Monday old Mr Fleming went collecting rents he was owed for various properties and managed to while away the hours chatting to the assorted tenants. His son had returned from Dunoon and had gone straight to his office. At four o'clock, the grandson, John Fleming bounded up the steps at number seventeen. He was amazed to see his grandfather taking a parcel in from the butcher, where he wondered, was Jess? It emerged that the door to Jess' room had been locked from the inside all weekend and old Mr Fleming explained that he had been unable to rouse her.

"It didn't occur to you that she might be dead?"
"Dead or not dead, she away!"

Old Mr Fleming's son, also called John, then arrived and the three men decided they had to get into the room. They discussed breaking the door down and then they noticed the pantry key in its lock - would this also fit the bedroom door? It did and they crowded in to the cold, dark room. Jess' body lay face down on the floor by her bed, she was naked but covered in a piece of carpet from the waist up. Blood soaked bed sheets were bundled onto the unmade bed.

"She's been laying there all this time - and me in the house!" shouted the old man.

Sauchiehall Street, Glasgow, in the 19th century

One of the Flemings ran to the butcher's shop and begged a Mr Train to fetch the police. He in turn ran off and bumped into the local doctor who came immediately. Dr Watson announced the obvious - that Jess was dead - and he took charge of proceedings. Outside, a small crowd gathered and PC Cameron was soon on the scene. News of screams, prostitutes and shadowy men was soon spilling from the lips of friends and neighbours. The only one who seems to have had little to say was old Mr Fleming. If the two Jess' aren't confusing enough, we now have the arrival of the police surgeon, Dr Fleming. He records the finding of an iron cleaver in a kitchen drawer, the discovery of three bloody footprints near the window, the loss of many of Jess' best clothes including a cinnamon coloured dress, and the fact that the corpse had been washed along with parts of the floor. The police soon established that the dead woman did not make the footprints and that silver cutlery was missing from the main house.

In the following days, much happened - the story hit the local newspapers but didn't fare well for column inches against the compelling story of a giant pineapple being put on public display, old Mr Fleming was arrested and the pawnbroker came forward with the items of silver marked 'F'. Jess McLachlan (or someone like her) took a trip to Hamilton where many witnesses observed her. James McLachlan happened to return from a long voyage and on reading the press reports commented to his wife that a woman wanted for questioning matched her description. Jess explained all - her friend had sent her items of stolen silver, clothes including a cinnamon dress to have dyed, and so on. Then she read of the murder, panicked and sent all the items left in a chest to be collected at Ayr Station. James agreed to bribe a railway official to get the chest sent to his sister's in Greenock as long as Jess would go to the police. A deal was struck and eventually, they sent the chest to the Sheriffs Court in Glasgow.

On what information or evidence the police first turned their attentions to Jess McLachlan we don't know, but it has been suggested that old Mr Fleming might have mentioned her name, and this is obviously quite likely. Anyway, the pawnbroker only knew her as 'McDonald' but he did have a description, which was published causing Mrs Campbell to raise the alarm. The police put a watch on Broomielaw and eventually both Jess and James McLachlan were bundled into a cab and driven off charged with theft and murder. Their child was given to Mrs Campbell for safekeeping.

Jess languished in Glasgow Prison as the police carried out searches of her home - over forty pawn tickets in a variety of names were discovered, torn clothing including a single sleeve from a brown dress and blood on the door lock. In Hamilton, a small girl found remnants of blood sodden rags tucked into bushes in a public park. Later police found a brown dress minus one sleeve! Meanwhile, Jess was asked to step into some bull's blood and make a footprint. It seemed to match those found in the dead woman's room.

The pre-trial of Jess McLachlan opened on Monday July 14th and almost immediately she was given the opportunity to explain her side of the story. She lied. She denied going to Sandyford Place at all, she claimed to have visited the friends with the sick child and she remembered returning home around midnight. Lies, lies, lies. That night she got talking to some fellow inmates and told them that she had worked for the Flemings and that old Mr Fleming would be found guilty of murder (he was still in custody) and that it was he who had brought the silver round for her to pawn. Meanwhile, James McLachlan was being released - the authorities now satisfied that he had been away from the country during the time the murder took place.

James returned to his sister's care and he shared with her his dark thoughts about his wife. Attentions then turned to the chest and it became clear that it had not arrived at the Sheriff's office. James went to the police and Superintendent McCall was sent to find the box. It turned up at Bridge Street Station where it had resided waiting for someone to pay the fourpence owed on it. The police opened it up and discovered a black silk dress, and two cloaks. The clothes had belonged to Jess McPherson and had been kept in a chest - this chest still sat at the murder scene, the remaining clothes having bloody handprints all over them.

The days of discussion went on. James joined the jostling crowds outside the court to catch a glimpse of his pale wife all too aware that his actions had sealed her fate. His sister came too but he sent her home, afraid that the police who swarmed over his home would question her about the handling of the chest. It was around this time that Jess McPherson was laid to rest, which further heightened tensions in the

Glasweigan press and public. On July 17th old Mr Fleming was freed and there seems a great deal of confusion surrounding the circumstances in which Jess was informed of this development - a fellow inmate claimed to have told her but her solicitors also took credit. Either way, at first Jess was jubilant - Fleming would now clear her name. Then hope turned to despair as he kept silent. Jess asked for James to visit her and he was dispatched to her lawyers - she wanted to talk with them.

Now, Jess' solicitors were eventually painted as being somewhat lax in their service to her - there were three of them and when Jess sent her message, two were away so it was left to a Mr Dixon to hurry to the cell. Jess told her story - the most detailed account of that night so far. Whatever she told him, Dixon was confounded. Until that moment he had believed her to be guilty, now he didn't know what to believe. Was she, as Jess was convinced, carrying the can because she was poor and old Mr Fleming rich?

The trial proper began on September 7th 1862, some three decades before prisoners were allowed to give evidence in court. Jess boasted to her fellow in-mates that she would stand up during old Mr Fleming's evidence and shout, "Was it me that did the deed?" and the shock would cause him to tell the truth. Her faith was never put to the test which is just as well as already, newspapers were bribing court officials for juicy tit-bits of gossip and the public was being prepared for a guilty verdict. The judge, who was known as 'Lord Death', was later described as con-

Glasgow's busy streets in the Victorian era

ducting the case, "as if putting his foot fiercely into one scale and kicking against the other!" In the square outside the court were the gallows - waiting.

Jess was charged with murder and theft. When old Mr Fleming eventually took the stand he was asked why, when the milk boy had called on the Saturday morning, he had been so quick to answer the door. Why hadn't he waited for Jess to do it as usual? His reply was stunning - "It was all over for her before then!". He later explained that he had gone to Jess' room and failing to gain admission, had knocked to wake her up. Despite the bloodstain in the lobby he hadn't been suspicious when she didn't appear for the weekend even though he knew she was being paid to look after him. He had decided not to call the police but to wait until his family returned on Monday night.

Dr Watson gave evidence detailing the injuries suffered by the victim and concluded that she had been struck several times with a blunt instrument - probably the cleaver - and that following a struggle the body had been dragged from the kitchen into the bedroom. Another witness of interest to us was Mrs Adams who did the odd bit of housework for Jess McLachlan. She recalled that her young daughter took the chest to the local station - it was to be conveyed to Hamilton. And finally, PC Campbell recounted tales of catching prostitutes and other loose women around Sandyford Place. He was asked to look at the prisoner - Jess actually stood up - and tell the court whether he had seen her on his patrols. He had not.

The case against Jess was summed up thus. On the charge of theft, the silver items had been in the Fleming house on Friday, old Mr Fleming had told them so, and they were pawned the following day by a woman matching Jess' description. Jess of course, claimed Mr Fleming had asked her to pawn them for him. The claim was that Jess had been at the house - her bloody footprints were found there - and she had taken some clothes. She had sought to have the cinnamon dress dyed and had dispatched some of the bloody garments, belonging to both women, to Hamilton Station. The defence, given at the end of the third consecutive eleven-hour day, was based on placing doubt in the jury's minds. Did they really believe that Jess had murdered her friend to gain some second-hand dresses? That she had killed and then spent the night at the murder scene? That old Mr Fleming hadn't wondered whether something strange had occurred? No, there was no proof the footprints were hers, they were similar that was all, there was no proof the silver - or the dresses - had even been in the house. There was no proof that Jess had been there at all. Could the jury really convict on the testimony of a mixed up, rather eccentric octogenarian? The court was adjourned.

The next day, Saturday September 20th, Jess begged her counsel to read out the most recent statement she had made - whether she was found guilty or not. At ten o'clock 'Lord Death' entered the court, he openly carried the black cap in his hand. His summing up has been recorded since as being wholly biased against Jess - he recounted the case, with some glaring inaccuracies. It took the jury nineteen minutes to find Jess McLachlan guilty.

The defence asked that Jess might be allowed to read a statement and she rose, pale and shaking but was unable to speak. Her counsel, Mr Rutherford Clark, took the paper from her hand. At ten past ten she had left her friends and made for Sandyford Place. Jess had answered the door and taken her to the kitchen explaining that the old man was still awake. Indeed, he was sitting at the kitchen table, which was laid with two sets of dishes. After a while he retired and the two women had a tot of rum each. Shortly afterwards and Fleming was back clutching a bottle of whiskey and a glass - there was a row about him drinking alone and not offering them any and Jess McPherson told him not to push her as she had a sharp tongue. He asked Jess to run out and buy him a pint, which she agreed to do but she found the shop shut. When she returned the door was locked and she had to go round to the back where the old man let her in. He explained that he had locked up to stop the local cats getting in. Then she saw Jess, lying on the floor covered in blood spots. She asked for water and cleaned her friend up, getting her into bed. She then cleaned the floor and asked Fleming to fetch a doctor. He refused and Jess managed to croak that she didn't want a fuss. Jess sat nursing her friend while the old man stood watching.

Eventually Jess confided in her friend that some days earlier old Fleming had come home drunk and tried to rape her. She had fought him off and they had reached some kind of truce but Fleming was scared of her. When Jess had gone to fetch the rum she had taunted the old man and he had struck her. Jess had collected her friend's clothes up to take with her so they could be washed. Towards dawn she had decided to go home and had gone to the front door but had found it locked. When she returned to the basement the old man was stood over Jess with the bloody cleaver in his hand. Jess was dead and Jess McLachlan screamed. Old Mr Fleming had hatched a plot - Jess should take the silver with her, he would make it look like a burglary and she should keep quiet - he would see her all right. So, Jess scurried off with the clothes and the silver and the rest, as they say, is history.

The court was stunned - the jury sat in silence and all eyes moved to Lord Deas. He picked up his black cap and sentenced Jess to hang. "And may God Almighty have mercy on your soul." As she was lead down she was just about heard to say, "Mercy! Aye, he'll have mercy for I'm innocent." Every street corner, every pub, every carriage was alive with discussions about the case. Many newspapers changed allegiance and called for Jess' release. Only the Glasgow Herald crowed about the verdict but they were not rewarded - crowds gathered outside their offices shouting and jeering. The Editor proclaimed them to be 'insane'. There was a flurry of claim and counter-claim, the lawyers were bribed, the judge was a fool, the Flemings were being protected by their own kind, Jess had been pregnant by old Mr Fleming - and much more besides. A petition was sent to the Home Secretary begging for a delay in carrying out the execution. At the same time James McLachlan emigrated with his sister, leaving his son with Jess' mother in Inverness. Well, Jess' execution was put on hold and as the years passed by so old Mr Fleming died, some of her lawyers also passed on and curiously, in 1892 a dying woman confessed to the murder but her claim was rejected.

Finally, in 1877, model prisoner 389/21 McLachlan was released. By now she was forty-four and had saved up thirty pounds. A cousin living in Greenock offered her a home and she attempted to start afresh but the local paper discovered her identity and hounded her out of the town. Not long after she emigrated to America with her son, where, it is believed, she met up with her husband. James died two years later and Jess married again. In 1899 her son wrote to the cousin in Greenock, "I am very sorry to let you know that my poor mother is dead. She died of pleurisy of the heart on New Year's morning." Nature had finally closed the case.

A CITY OF VICE, CON-MEN AND SWINDLERS
A Manchester policeman's lot

VICTORIAN Manchester was notorious as a centre for vice, con-men and swindlers, and according to Jerome Caminada, a policeman who rose from constable to superintendent in a 30 year police career, the worse areas for crime and particularly vice were Spinning Field, Hardman Street, Dolefield and surrounding alleyways on the Manchester and Salford boundary.

Jerome Caminada

Ironically, it was Bootle Street, until recent years a street housing the headquarters of the Manchester City Police, which was one of the worse dens for prostitution and theft.

In these thoroughfares, according to Caminada, the women were the most degraded class, and their chief victims were drunken men, collier lads and country 'flats' or 'yokels' whom they picked and rifled with impunity. Public houses with such names as the 'Dog and Rat', the 'Red, White and Blue', 'the Old Ship', the 'Pat M'Carthy' and the 'Green Man' were noted for their criminal fraternity, and it was a very brave police officer who entered these premises without fearing for his safety.

Passing these alehouses the pedestrian could hear the sound of mechanical organs, drums and tambourines, and upon entering the sight was usually one of youths and girls assembled in a room furnished with a few wooden forms and tables.

The women, 'unfortunates' as Victorian society called prostitutes, lived on the premises and the proprietor made extra income from their sordid trade. Some rude attempt would be made at an indecent song by a half-drunken girl trying to impress a hardy collier lad, but more often than not incessant quarrelling and the obscene language of her companions drowned the songs.

The policeman's lot was certainly not a happy one in those days, and most of the notorious public houses employed a man to watch for the police approaching on his beat. Caminada himself claimed in his autobiography *25 Years of Detective Life* that during his career he helped to put an end to over 400 such places!

'Bullies' or 'Coshers' were another kind of criminal who preyed upon the unsuspecting Manchester visitor. They got hold of some girl, who they compelled by fear to act as an 'unfortunate', and when she accosted and decoyed her victim to a convenient spot, the 'Cosher' would appear and rob him of all his belongings, in many cases garrotting him, and if the victim showed any opposition he was very badly beaten. Deansgate in the 1860s was a noted place for prize fighting, and in several beer-

Deansgate in the 1890s

houses there were regular bouts. When this was stopped the fights were continued in the kitchens, stables, cellars and any other place where the police were unlikely to appear. Many of the same beerhouses also put on dog fights, 'drawing the badger' and 'sports' such as rat baiting.

In Caminada's time public houses were allowed to stay open from 4am to 1am, so it is clear that for 21 hours each day a considerable amount of time was spent in entertaining the criminal classes or criminals planning their next 'heist'.

Another 'haunt of iniquity', Caminada said, was the neighbourhood of Canal Street, Minshull Street, Richmond Street and back Piccadilly. These plague spots were notorious for recruiting the more middle-class type of criminal and many a clerk, or other 'respectable' young man, began his criminal career by pilfering from his employer's till.

Sentences for criminal offences were particularly punitive and even Caminada, a robust character, was astonished at the severity of some punishments. He cited cases he had known when men had been sentenced to 14 years penal servitude for stealing 2d, while another was jailed for 10 years for stealing a pair of boots, a hat and linen jacket to the total value of 12 shillings (60p). Two men were jailed for seven years for stealing a halfpenny while, hypocritically, another man was jailed for only 12 months for stealing £4000. Another example of Victorian class distinction.

Caminada wrote: " I have often stood by when men have been sentenced to terms of penal servitude which have filled me with sorrow, because I have been convinced that in many cases the sentence meant either a criminal death of insanity; for astonishing as the statement may appear, I have never yet known a man or woman return from a long sentence of penal servitude in their rational mind; and yet in all probability the criminal had never in the course of his or her life a single chance of getting out of the circumstances in which he or she was born, breathing through poverty an air of temptation." It was an astonishingly liberal attitude for the stern Victorian era, and particularly for a policeman of the time.

Caminada who had joined the Manchester force in 1868, was also a

The World of Crime

man of unwitting humour and in volume one of his memoirs, published in 1895, he wrote: "One night whilst on duty, in uniform, in John Dalton Street, Deansgate, in the year 1868, I was called by some person and on turning around to answer my usual 'Yes Sir', I was asked by some individual, in terms none too polite, 'Have I to pay rates and taxes to keep such lazy fellows as you walking around the streets?' Without further ceremony or warning he gave me a blow on my nose, which made me reel; but when I turned upon him he took to his heels and ran into a beerhouse in Ridgefield.

"I was certainly a little nonplussed. To get a violent blow on the nose at 10.30pm on a cold March night, was not a very pleasant experience for a beginner, especially as the air was keen, and frozen snow was lying on the ground."

He walked away from the beerhouse door to return to his John Dalton

Above: Market Street, Manchester, pictured in the 1890s, a scene well known to Caminada

Right: Jerome Caminada photographed at the height of his detective career

Street patrol when, without the slightest of warning he received a blow on the ear and a voice exclaimed 'Take that! How do you like it!' Caminada wrote "I didn't like it at all" and turning round he recognised the same man who had hit him on the nose. He chased the man and caught him, and later recorded "In the scuffle he managed to get my hand in his mouth, and began to bite away in a right good fashion. Fortunately, he had no teeth, but he worked away so vigorously with his gums that I could feel the pain for weeks after!"

Caminada retired in 1899, after reaching the dizzy heights of superintendent and becoming the most honoured policeman in the force that then totalled 1,037 men.

THE REAL SHERLOCK HOLMES
The criminal links of Sir Arthur Conan Doyle

SIR Arthur Conan Doyle, creator of fiction's most famous detective - Sherlock Holmes, enjoyed a colourful reputation.

Born in Scotland, Doyle was the very essence of the British country gent - sincere, kind, enthusiastic, and with a passion for learning. Although he achieved fame through his literary creation, Doyle was also something of a celebrity in scientific and media circles. He used this to great effect, often championing causes he held close to his heart - he argued for reforms to the divorce laws, promoted spiritualism and even campaigned against alleged British atrocities in the Congo.

Conan Doyle as a young man

Because of his renown as a crime writer Doyle often received mail from readers begging him to investigate real cases, which occasionally, he did. On one occasion he alerted police to the links between two crimes reported in the newspapers and in another he took the side of a dog accused of killing sheep. In 1906 he was widowed and is said to have suffered depression, spending much of his time in his native Scotland. It was during this period that he received a letter regarding one George Edalji, a vicar's son from Great Wyrley in the West Midlands. The Reverend Edalji had moved to Britain from India and joined the Church of England - an Indian vicar was something of a curiosity and the family had suffered repeated racial abuse, death threats and the like.

The local police were convinced that the threats were being made by young George himself. In 1903 there were a number of incidents in the

The Lusitania, the ship used by Oscar Slater, was sunk in 1915

area of cattle having their stomachs slashed and an anonymous letter sent to the police pointed the finger at George Edalji! He was arrested and charged. The court was given evidence by a handwriting expert called Thomas Gurrin and George was found guilty. Whilst he was away serving time another cow was attacked and a second letter sent to the police. They were unmoved surmising that the attacks were part of a bizarre religious ceremony and the fresh incident had been carried out by one of George's followers. The public, however, were not convinced and a campaign was launched for George's release.

In October 1906 a ten thousand-name petition was sent to the Home Secretary. George was released but the conviction was not over-turned and there was no official word on why he had been set free. The case was big news and Doyle visited the scene of the crime and spent time with George. He noticed that the boy had poor eye-sight and deduced that it would be nigh on impossible for him to find cattle in the dark, let alone carry out delicate knife work on them, he discredited the handwriting expert who had already sent one innocent man to prison and he found further discrepancies with evidence. Although the conviction was never over-turned, thanks largely to Doyle's endorsement of his innocence, George Edalji was allowed to continue with his life.

The second notable case which Doyle became embroiled in was that of the murder of Marion Gilchrist. Like all great crime fiction this took place against an evocative backdrop - a bitterly cold December in Glasgow. The year was 1908. Gilchrist had been enjoying an evening at home, sharing the company of her paid companion. The companion had been sent out for ten minutes to fetch an errand and on her return found her employer dead in a pool of blood and surrounded by scattered papers and jewellery. As she had approached the house a man had rushed past her - was this the murderer?

Oscar Slater was a European born petty thief who pawned a brooch not long after the crime. He then boarded the *Lusitania* under a fake identity and left Scotland for America. The police named him as the chief suspect and he was arrested on arrival in New York and deported. The brooch proved not to have been stolen from Miss Gilchrist's, Slater had been with his mistress and her servant at the time of the murder, and the police coached witnesses to falsely identify him as the culprit. Nevertheless Slater was found guilty and sentenced to hang.

Once again, there was a public outcry and a large petition handed to the Home Secretary. Arthur Conan Doyle was alerted to the case and it was he who discovered that Slater had checked into a Liverpool hotel using his real name the night before boarding the ship. He had only used a false name on board because he was leaving with his mistress to start a new life and did not want his wife to trace him. Doyle published, in 1912, a booklet detailing the case and campaigning for Slater's release. Questions were asked in the House of Commons and new evidence was uncovered - another witness to Slater's alibi and the fact that the paid companion had named the man who had brushed against her that night - and it was not Slater!

This new evidence fell on deaf ears and although the execution was cancelled, Oscar Slater remained in prison with no idea of the campaign to free him. Fifteen years later, Slater managed to smuggle out a letter begging for someone to re-open the case. Doyle once more took up the cause and for the next couple of years wrote many letters to influential friends. In 1927 he collaborated with a local journalist on a book that re-told the story and suggested that Miss Gilchrist must have known her assailant as she had obviously let him into the house. Furthermore they urged the companion to speak up and they suggested that they knew the killer's identity.

This volume opened up another can of worms with newspapers carrying out a bidding war for further revelations. Within months Slater was free but not pardoned. Doyle updated his booklet and sent a copy to the MP for Dumfriesshire, John Charteris, who was also Miss Gilchrist's nephew. Doyle assisted in raising funds to fight an appeal but, when the money was there, Slater announced he was not minded to go back to court. Doyle was furious but Slater was found innocent on a technicality anyway.

No one was ever found guilty of Gilchrist's murder but we now know that Doyle's prime suspect was none other than Francis Charteris, the victim's nephew and a professor at Saint Andrew's University. Although he never did publicly announce his thoughts, Doyle's sending of the book to Charteris' brother was a warning – he was being watched. We can only speculate as to whether, had Charteris been poor and less well connected, the matter would have been handled differently.

Harry's hypocrisy!

In the aftermath of the First World War mediums and psychics saw business booming, such was the number of widows and mothers who had lost their loved ones and were desperate for news 'from the other side'. Amongst the more famous mediums of the day were Eva C. (an Algerian who had previously gone under the name Marthe Beraud until a scandal had caused her to adopt a new identity), Margery (otherwise known as Mrs Mina Crandon) and one Lady Jean Conan Doyle, wife of Sir Arthur.

For as many believers there were equal numbers of disbelivers. One of the most famous of these, who set himself the task of unmasking the unscrupulous, was Ehrich Weiss who also revelled in a stage name – Harry Houdini. He would disguise himself in a wig and sometimes, a false beard, to attend seances only to halt the evening and expose the trickery involved. All very worthy but .... wasn't he himself involved in the same type of business?

A DOUBLE MURDERESS?

The case of Lizzie Borden

THE small town of Fall River, Massachusetts, about 60 miles south of Boston, has become the centre of a macabre tourist industry - thanks to the killings of husband and wife Andrew and Abby Borden in their home at 92 Second Street, on August 4th, 1892, and the subsequent arrest and trial of Andrew's youngest daughter Lizzie Borden. Today it is possible not only to visit the house, but to stay overnight in the very rooms in which the the murders took place!

The bed and breakfast arrangement has been made to cope with the demand of tourists who visit this town to see for themselves the scenes of crime with the same enthusiasm as those who longed to see the house more than a century ago. Erected in 1845 in what has been described as a "Greek revival style", the Borden house has been a city landmark ever since, and while today's guests can savour their breakfast of bananas and coffee, jonny-cakes, sugar cookies and more tradtional breakfast staples, that the owners describe as "similar to the one the Bordens ate of the morning of the murders", the more sensitive cannot fail to be moved by the tragic events that took place in that property on that hot August day so long ago.

Fall River in 1892 was a thriving business community and the world's largest cotton cloth manufacturing centre, ideally situated as it was (and is) between Boston and Canada to the north and bustling New York City to the south. It was in this thriving community that the Borden family had prospered, at one time being one of the largest property owners in the town, and it was here that Andrew Borden was still a pillar of the community and a man of influence and wealth.

On the morning of August 4th, Andrew Borden, described in some accounts as a humourless man who had worked himself up from being an undertaker to director of a textile mill, and eventually president of the town's bank, had returned home at about 10.40 am after a brief visit to look at his various business ventures. He had been feeling ill for the past couple of days with a severe stomach ache and he decided to have a lie down. He had been greeted at the door by the family maid, Bridget Sullivan, who later said she had noticed Lizzie Borden at the top of the stairs as she fumbled to open the door for her employer. As Andrew entered the house Lizzie came downstairs and said to her father: "Mrs Borden has gone out. She had a note from somebody who is sick."

Nodding to his daughter, and apparently unmoved by Lizzie referring to his wife as "Mrs Borden" since she was not on friendly terms with her stepmother Abby, Andrew made his way to his bedroom using the back stairs leading from the kitchen area. A few minutes later, however, he returned downstairs and went to lie on the couch in the sitting room. Ten minutes later, at 11am, Bridget, who had also been suffering from the same stomach complaint as her employer and had earlier been sick in the garden, also decided to lie down, but she had been on her bed less that ten minutes when she was disturbed by a cry from Lizzie.

"Come down quick! Father's dead! Somebody came in and killed him!" Lizzie shouted. Within a few minutes the local doctor arrived, the police had been called, and the Bordens' next door neighbour Mrs Churchill came over to see what was happening. Bridget, though obviously in a state of shock, nevertheless had the presence of mind to ask Lizzie where she had been when her father was being killed.

"I was out in the back yard," Lizzie said, "and heard a groan and came in, and the screen door was wide open."

When Mrs Churchill asked her the same question, Lizzie had told her she was in the barn when she heard her father's cry.

As the family's GP, Dr. Bowen, examined Andrew's body and covered it with a sheet, Lizzie commented to Bridget that she was sure she had heard her stepmother come in the house and go upstairs, and ordered the traumatised maid to go and look. Bridget asked Mrs Churchill to accompany her and as the pair climbed the front stairs they were confronted with a scene of pure horror, for lying face forward on the floor of the guest bedroom was the battered body of Abby Borden.

Dr. Bowen swiftly climbed the stairs as the maid and the neighbour shouted out, and his examination of Mrs Borden's corpse revealed that she had died of repeated attacks from behind, and further revealed that she had 19 wounds in the back of her head and neck, while a large flap of flesh had been sliced from her skull. But what was particularly revealing about his examination was the news that blood around and on the body was already congealed and dark, thus offering the obvious conclusion that she had been killed some time before her husband.

Dr. Bowen's examination of Andrew had shown that he had been killed where he lay on the couch, with no evidence of a struggle. He had suffered a devastating attack by his slayer, and his body had 11 deep blows to his face that had caused his eyeball to be split from its socket and had severed his nose. Blood was still seeping from his wounds at the time of the doctor's examination.

Police searched the house and found two complete axes and two hatchets in the cellar, and a further hatchet which was coated with coal ash on both sides and with a freshly broken handle in a wooden box, and they quickly assumed the latter to be the murder weapon. A double autopsy was carried out on the Bordens' bodies on the dining room table in 92 Second Street, and for some reason the bodies remained in the house overnight each covered with a sheet. Bizarrely, Lizzie also stayed in the house overnight in the company of her sister Emma, a 42 years old spinster, who had been staying with friends 15 miles away in Fairhaven, until she was summoned home by the tragedy. The maid Bridget was too frightened to remain in the house and stayed overnight with a neighbour never to return.

Andrew Borden's body (Pic courtesy of Fall River Herald News)

Two days after the double murder there was a double funeral for Andrew and Abby Borden, each of whom was buried minus their skull which had been removed by the pathologist for further tests. This information was kept secret from the mourners and the evidence gained from the examination of the heads would later be produced in court.

Lizzie later told investigators that she had been in the house at the time her stepmother was killed, though she had neither seen or heard anything. She said she thought Abby had gone out in response to receiving the message about her sick friend, though no sign was ever found of the alleged note, and the prosecutor claimed it had never existed. The investigators also looked into Lizzie's claim that she had been in the barn. She elaborated by saying she had spent about 20 minutes in the hayloft looking for a box of lead sinkers which were used

Abby Borden's body (Pic Courtesy of Fall River Herald

The World of Crime

Right: The Borden home in Fall River, pictured in 1992. Today this house is a Bed and Breakfast establishment, and guests can stay in the very rooms in which the murders took place!

Below: Maplecroft, Fall River, where Lizzie and Emma Borden later went to live

for fishing. But a detective later claimed he looked in the hayloft but saw no footprints in the thick dust that was lying heavily on the floor, though his own shoes did leave an impression.

Further evidence was soon produced by police who found that the day before the killings Lizzie had tried to buy poison from a local druggist. In such a small community it was easy to establish that Lizzie was the person who had tried to make the purchase of what was regarded as one of the quickest poisons around, and the same night she had confided in a friend that she predicted something was about to happen at her home. Three days after the murders Lizzie also allegedly burnt a dress in the kitchen stove, though she handed over a silk dress to police after claiming she was wearing it on the day of the murders. It was a claim that was later rejected after the court heard that no lady in Lizzie's position would wear a silk dress in the early morning when she was carrying out chores and visiting a filthy hayloft.

The Borden family graves in Fall River Cemetery

The grave of Andrew and Abby Borden, Fall River

Although the police felt they had enough evidence to arrest and charge Lizzie with the double murders, which they did on August 11th, 1892, her friends felt it was impossible that someone from such a background and as well bred as Lizzie could carry out such a dastardly act. They pointed out the lack of bloodstains on her clothing or person, though opponents claimed the dress she burnt must have contained enough blood stains to warrant the deliberate act of burning the garment. Nobody in Fall River, it seemed, could determine whether Lizzie Borden had committed the crimes or not, and even today the pros and cons continue to be debated.

But whatever the feelings among her neighbours and friends in Fall River, a Grand Jury who heard the outline presented by prosecutors in November of that year decided there was a case to answer and 20 out of 21 jurors voted for her indictment on the charge of murdering her father and stepmother.

On Monday, June 5th, 1893, ten months after the killings, Lizzie's trial started in the small, square brick courthouse of the Massachusetts Superior Court in New Bedford, and the New York Sun ran an editorial comment on that opening day which proclaimed: "She is either the most injured of innocents or the blackest of monsters. She either hacked her father and stepmother to pieces with the furious brutality of the ogre in Poe's story of the Rue Morgue or some other person did it and she suffers the double torture of losing her parents and being wrongfully accused of their murders."

Under the rules of the Superior Court in Massachusetts at that time, all murder cases were heard in front of three judges, and in the Borden case the outstanding publicity meant that Albert Mason, the Chief Justice, decided to assign himself to the case alongside associates Justin Dewy and Caleb Blodgett. He also ordered alterations to the courtroom to cater for the demand, and in the process allowed 219 seats instead of the customary 182. The court later had to make further alterations to cater for press representatives from around the world.

Massachusetts Attorney General Arthur E. Pillsbury should have been the normal choice to be prosecutor in such a major crime which carried the possibility of the death penalty, but he decided to take a vacation to Florida instead and District Attorney Hosea M. Knowlton was appointed to lead the case for the State, assisted by William H. Moody, a fellow District Attorney for the East of the City. Knowlton was not keen to take on the case, but Moody had a reputation for dogged perseverance and efficiency, (he later became US Attorney General), so the contrasting styles of the two men would themselves act as a dramatic backdrop to the court case.

Knowlton struck the opening notes of the case with the words: "Upon the fourth day of August of last year, an old man and woman, husband and wife, were severally killed by unlawful human agency." Moody addressed the jury with his announcement of intent, which means he outlined the prosecution's case against Lizzie Borden, reviewing the scene of crime, and pointing out the ill-feeling that evidently existed between Lizzie and her stepmother. He also mentioned the attempt by Lizzie to buy poison, and told the jury: "I think, gentlemen, you will be satisfied that there can be no question that the person who made this application for this deadly poison was the prisoner."

On the claim made by Lizzie that her stepmother had left the house in answer to a note from a friend, Moody, who strongly resembled Theodore Roosevelt, said: "That, gentlemen, we put to you as a lie, intended for no purpose except to stifle inquiry into the whereabouts of Mrs Borden." He went on to cry down Lizzie's claim that she had been in the loft, pointing out that no footprints had been noted by detectives, and claimed that Lizzie had burnt the dress she wore on the morning of the murders in the kitchen stove to remove incriminating evidence.

He ended his announcement with the words: The time for idle rumour, for partial, insufficient information, for hasty and inexact reasoning, is past!"

Throughout all this Lizzie sat ill at ease, though there was a start of horror and amazement on her face during Moody's outline when he apparently accidentally uncovered the two skulls of Andrew and Abby Borden that lay on the bench in front of the prosecution team.

When Bridget Sullivan took the stand she told the court that on the morning of the murders she had risen at about 6.15am as usual but had a headache and was feeling unwell, though she said carried out her usual pre-breakfast chores. She also asked Lizzie if she wanted any breakfast, but the accused said she would get her own coffee and cookies and as she started getting her food Bridget went outside to be sick. She claimed she was in the rear yard of the property for about 10 or 15 minutes before returning to the house again, by which time Lizzie was nowhere to be seen.

Bridget added: "Mrs Borden was in the dining room as I was fixing my dining room table, and she asked me if I had anything to do that morning. I said, No, not particular, if she had anything for me to do. She said she wanted the windows washed. I asked her how and she said inside and outside, they are awful dirty." This, claimed Bridget, was the last time she saw Mrs Borden alive.

Throughout the trial the prosecution tried, with considerable success, to paint a picture of a household in disharmony and being in a somewhat neurotic state, and one that was particularly fearful that the house was being watched by anonymous prowlers and business enemies of Andrew Borden. It was also a house, prosecutors claimed, that was at war with itself, meaning almost continuous conflict between Lizzie and Emma Borden, and their stepmother.

Medical evidence offered to the court showed that Abby had died a full ninety minutes before Andrew, and William H. Moody again uncovered their skulls, though this time deliberately, and demonstrated that the hatchet head found in the Borden home and suspected of being the murder weapon fitted the indentations in the skulls perfectly!

More and more evidence was put forward, but one particularly important potential witness, Eli Bence, the drug store assistant, who was expected to offer positive identification of Lizzie as the person attempting to buy poison, was objected to by defence counsel George D. Robinson on the grounds that his appearance was "irrelevant".

The three man defence team cross-examined prosecution witnesses and produced their own outline of the case, including various witnesses who claimed they had seen people loitering in the vicinity of the Borden home, though no positive identification was given. Emma, too, was brought to the stand in what many observers believed was a well rehearsed performance, though prosecutor Moody and his team managed to fluster her during their own cross-examinations.

Ironically, the main defence witness, Lizzie Borden, was not called to the stand, and her defence team made a brief final argument in what can only be called a singular style by offering the jury, made up of local farmers, a sentimental choice of either releasing Lizzie by finding

The World of Crime

**Above:
Lizzie Borden
pictured in
middle age**

**Right:
Lizzie's modest
grave in Fall River
Cemetery**

her not guilty, or finding her guilty and having her sentenced to death. The result was perhaps inevitable in a small community that did not want to have a trial (of one of their own) in the first place. On June 21st, 1893, Lizzie was acquitted of the double murders and released to great cheering from the gathered crowd. In tears and close to collapse she said simply "Take me home."

The Borden case has continued to fascinate investigators and public alike, and there are many who still believe that Lizzie Borden was a killer whose conviction was impossible in such a close knit community where everyone knew everyone else and no one could accept that a woman, particularly one who was even described by District Attorney Knowlton as "A Christian lady", could be capable of such a heinous crime.

But whatever the truth, the legend of Lizzie Borden has gone into criminal history, and also produced an epitaph of infamy in the verse:

> "Lizzie Borden took an axe
> And gave her mother 40 whacks:
> When she saw what she had done
> She gave her father 41"

But did she?

THE 'BRIDES IN THE BATH'
George Joseph Smith

BORN in 1872 in London's Bethnal Green, George Joseph Smith spent much of his formative years on the wrong side of the law. There were several short terms in prison for burglary, receiving stolen goods and other such charges. Indeed, by the age of 25, in 1897, Smith was known as a regular at Wormwood Scrubs. It was in this year that he found himself being released after yet another term of incarceration and he took the opportunity to relocate to Leicester where he opened a bakers under the name George Oliver Love.

Smith wasn't a businessman but he did have a taste for the highlife and a pretty woman. It didn't take him long to find the latter – within weeks of moving to Leicester he had met and married Caroline Thornhill and after the bakery closed due to financial problems they left for London where he promised her a belated honeymoon. The poor girl was in for a shock though – upon arrival he made her take a position as a housemaid to generate some badly needed income. But it wasn't enough and Smith persuaded his bride to begin stealing from her employers to supplement her wages. Eventually they relocated to Eastbourne.

It was here that things turned sour for Mrs Love – she tried to sell some silverware to a pawnbroker who became suspicious and the police were called. Caroline was charged but her husband made off and left her to face the music alone. Although the court was told that Caroline had been heavily influenced by Love, she was found guilty and sentenced to twelve months in prison. Whilst all this was going on, George was back in London where he bigamously married his landlady in order to secure rent-free accommodation.

In 1900 Caroline was released from prison and George amazingly had the gall to write to her and beg for reconciliation – she wisely ignored the letter but soon bumped into him whilst on a visit to the capital. The police were called and he was arrested. In 1901 he was sentenced to two years hard labour for receiving stolen goods. Upon his release he discovered that Caroline had emigrated to Canada however, they were never divorced and she was to remain his only legal wife. Smith returned to his landlady 'wife' for a short period before setting out on a tour of the south coast and the West Country. During his travels he managed to con £90 from a lonely spinster in Brighton and it was with this money that he opened a second-hand furniture store in Bristol in 1908. Here he met and married Edith Pegler whom he installed as his housekeeper as he travelled the country. Poor Edith was convinced Smith was away on business, however the evil conman was preying on other women. In Southampton he met and married Sarah Freeman – she believed him to be an antiques expert named George Rose. They moved to Clapham and within a week he had taken control of her entire fortune - £300. One day he took Sarah to the National Gallery where he asked her to wait on a bench whilst he went to the lavatory – he never returned and when she arrived home she found the flat stripped and her husband gone.

His next victim was young Beatrice 'Bessie' Mundy who again lost her life savings after just a couple of weeks of marriage. About a year after Smith had walked out on Bessie she decided to start a new life and moved to Weston-Super-Mare. In an extraordinary turn of fate – who should she see walking along the promenade? – George Smith, or as Bessie knew him, Henry Williams. Mr Williams explained to his wife that he had been searching the country for her and had discovered her move to the seaside town and had followed her there. The couple were re-united and Bessie went back to George's lodgings with him. The landlady didn't believe the story for a minute and she sent word to Bessie's aunt that trouble was brewing. By the time help arrived, the young couple had gone – to Kent. Here they drew up new wills leaving their fortunes to each other. Smith of course, had nothing to leave but Bessie was worth over £2,000. Their new home lacked a bath and Mr Williams was insistent that they should have one – he even sent his wife to haggle over the price at the local ironmongers and eventually, for £2, one was purchased. Shortly after, the doctor was called and Williams explained that his wife had passed out during a fit. The doctor brought her round and gave the couple a quantity of sedative. Bessie wrote to her family telling them how happy she was and disclosed the content of her new will! Within days she was dead having drowned in the bath whilst her husband was out buying herrings for breakfast. Mr Williams inherited £2,500, had his wife buried as cheaply as possible and took the bath back to the suppliers for a refund.

By 1913 he was living in Southsea and was now using his real name – George Smith. Here he married pretty Alice Burnham and within days of the wedding insured her life for £500. Two days later and they were off on honeymoon to Blackpool, Smith having taken charge of his wife's finances. Smith wanted nothing but the best for his bride – in fact, he insisted they stay in a more expensive boarding house – one with the luxury of a bath. Alice wrote to her family saying she was having a lovely time although she had been suffering from headaches. One morning Mr Smith set out to buy eggs for breakfast, the boarding house owners noticed a patch of water on their living room ceiling and …

well, the pattern continued. Alice was found dead in her bath, a verdict of accidental death was filed, Smith inherited £600 and a cheap funeral was booked and paid for.

In Bournemouth he was Charles Oliver Smith and in 1914 Alice Reavil was taken up the aisle. She financed the opening of an antiques shop, which quickly headed into debt then one day the couple took a walk in the park where he left her. She never saw him or her savings again. Within months Margaret Lofty married a John Lloyd in, ironically, Bath. Mr and Mrs Lloyd moved to Highgate in London – taking lodgings, which included a bath. On their first evening the landlady heard loud splashing in the bathroom above her then organ music then Mr Lloyd going out for some supper. Tragically, Mrs Lloyd was found drowned in her bath later that evening, was buried in a common grave and her husband inherited her savings.

Mr Lloyd reverted to Mr Smith and returned to Bristol where his wife, Edith was still running the second-hand furniture shop for him. Then things started to become difficult for Mr Smith – the *News of the World* ran a large feature on the mystery surrounding Mrs Lloyd's death in Highgate. Alice Burnham's father and a Mr Haynes in Blackpool both read the article and recognised similarities. Both men alerted Scotland Yard who began a surveillance operation that led to his arrest in 1915. Several bodies were exhumed, under

Exhuming one of the victims

the watchful eye of pathologist Bernard Spilsbury, and on 23rd March Smith was charged with three murders.

The trial began in June with Smith proclaiming his innocence throughout. He even started shouting insults at those who testified against him including Caroline Thornhill. But despite the valiant efforts of his counsel, Edward Marshall Hall, they were unable to compete with the brilliant theatrical act of Bernard Spilsbury re-enacting the alleged method of murder using a bath and a live volunteer. In fact, so realistic was the scene that the girl being used almost drowned! It took just 22 minutes for the jury to find Smith guilty and he was taken to Pentonville Prison where he quickly broke down and gradually lost his looks and stylish manner.

Bernard Spilsbury

Smith was one of the first murderers to use the new appeal court and it was here that he made a last appearance, immaculately dressed and with his trademark moustache neatly waxed. He was to be disappointed however when the Lord Chief Justice upheld the original verdict. Smith, clutching the hand rail, was finally a broken man. He was taken to Maidstone where he was to be hung. The night before the execution Smith was asked whether he wished to confess but he declined – he did however spend some time talking about Edith Pegler and how much money he would be leaving to her. Edith had tried to visit him on several occasions but he had refused her.

On 13th August 1915, just after breakfast, Smith was led to the gallows. As the trapdoor opened to carry him to his death, he shouted one last sentence, "I'm innocent!".

THE SALE OF THE CENTURY!
How some of the world's most famous landmarks came up for sale

IN 1925 five respected French businessmen were invited to meet with Count Victor Lustig on a matter of national security - a matter which was deemed 'top secret'. Lustig confided in them that the Eiffel Tower was in a dangerous state of repair and was to be pulled down. The men were invited, in strictest confidence, to submit tenders for the demolition and removal of the resulting 7,000 tons of scrap metal.

Lustig had in fact already chosen the man for the job, a man desperate to break into Parisian society, Andre Poisson. Poisson was invited back and tipped off that the Count intended to give him the lucrative contract providing that the businessman would be willing to provide a back-hander. Poisson had a banker's draft made over to Lustig and sat back waiting for the contract to put him on the map.

Meanwhile, Lustig and his accomplice left the country - he wasn't a count, the Eiffel Tower wasn't about to collapse, and there was no contract. The con was so effective that he even used it again, selling the Tower to a second scrap metal merchant. In fact, Lustig who was Czechoslovakian by birth, had used over twenty aliases and worked his way across Europe with various scams - being arrested almost fifty times!

Victor Lustig emigrated to America where he carried out another selection of cons including selling banknote duplicators at $25,000 a go. Needless to say, they didn't work! Eventually Lustig fell in with Al Capone, in fact he tried to con him but thought better of it! In 1945 he was found guilty of distributing $134,000,000 worth of counterfeit bills and sentenced to twenty years, part of which he served in Alcatraz. He died in 1947 in Springfield Prison, Missouri.

Al Capone

Remember when Lustig sold the Eiffel Tower? - 1925. Over in London, in the same year, a Scot named Arthur Furguson was doing the same thing. Furguson was a former actor who had in fact played an American conned by a trickster in a stage play. He gave up acting and moved to London where he decided to put into practise what he'd seen on the stage.

Arthur would wait at famous tourist attractions until a passing traveller engaged him in conversation. He would explain that Britain was in serious debt due to the cost of the Great War and that the government had announced that some of the great monuments were to be sold off to raise cash. The tourists would be drawn in by his tale and then Furguson would announce that that was what he was doing there, paying homage to the soon to be lost history of a great country but as the man charged with arranging the disposal he had to carry out the dreadful deed.

Nelson's Column was 'sold' for £6,000

Now, you would think people would have just nodded and walked on...but oh no! A man on holiday from Iowa wrote him a cheque for £6,000 to buy Nelson's Column and have it shipped home, he sold Big Ben for £1,000 and he got £2,000 for Buckingham Palace! It was such a successful year that he

Top: 'Big Ben', the famous clock tower of the Houses of Parliament in London was 'bought' for £1,000 by an American tourist

Right: The Statue of Liberty was priced at $100,000 by conman Arthur Ferguson, who also tried to rent the White House (below) for a further $100,000 a year!

could afford to emigrate so off he went to America.

Within a month he found himself stood outside the White House where he entered into conversation with a Texan millionaire farmer. The farmer was impressed by the presidential pile and spoke of his desire to own somewhere just like it. He'd met the right person, hadn't he! Furguson explained that the chap was in luck, the government were looking for ways to cut costs and had decided to rent out the White House. And lo and behold, Furguson was the agent charged with finding new tenants. A deal was struck and the farmer agreed to rent the mansion for $100,000 a year. He even put down the deposit!

In New York an Australian tourist was regaled with secret development plans for the harbour which sadly meant that the Statue of Liberty was having to be dismantled and sold. But wait a minute! - wasn't it just what Sydney Harbour needed! The tourist, a businessman, was thrilled at his luck and he took a celebratory picture of Furguson posing with the Statue. It was the Scot's first, and last, mistake and when the Australian tried to raise the cash needed to buy, $100,000, his bank became suspicious and the police were alerted. Armed with a photo of the con-man they began a search and eventually he was taken into custody.

Furguson served just five years and upon release declared that he was turning his back on crime, mind you, there was little left to sell and anyway, he had amassed a small fortune. He lived out his last years in California, dying in 1938.

THE AGONY OF AGATHA...

The romance of the roaring twenties - bright young things heading off to the Riviera, the Flappers, the Charleston, Art Deco - what a wonderfully colourful decade! And what a time for murder and mystery!

In December 1926, the young wife of Colonel Archibald Christie disappeared. Her Morris Cowley car being found abandoned by a waterlogged chalk-pit, it's headlights left burning bright. Meanwhile, in Harrogate, a Mrs Teresa Neele was checking into her hotel, visiting Great Britain on her first trip from South Africa. Colonel Christie was under suspicion but little did the police know that Teresa Neele was really one Mrs Agatha Christie. Soon the couple were reunited, Agatha claiming a bout of depression for her disappearance. Friends told a different story but did Agatha set the whole thing up for publicity - or to stop her husband's affairs? It was one mystery Britain's Who-dunnit author took to her grave.

Agatha Christie

Abney Hall where Christie stayed

H.H. HOLMES
The monster of 63rd Street

NUMBER 1316 Callowhill Street, a few blocks north of City Hall in Philadelphia, USA, was a two-storey house of no particular architectural interest, but to local carpenter Eugene Smith the building could possibly represent a brighter future, for he had been advised to visit its occupant whose lettered sign on his door read 'B.F. Perry, Patents Bought and Sold'. For Eugene, a modest man, had invented a new saw-set which could sharpen saws with much less effort than was usual, and he hoped to patent the invention and make his fortune.

Meeting Mr. Perry, a tall, dark, bony man with a wispy moustache, Eugene explained the invention and Perry expressed enough interest to ask to see a model. Perry then asked: "In the meantime, how about doing a few carpentry jobs for me in the house?"

"Sure," Smith replied. "I'd be glad to earn a few extra dollars."

On August 22nd, while hard at work in the property, Smith saw a man enter the house and go up to a room on the upper floor with Perry, but thought nothing more about it. A few days later he called back at Callowhill Street to ask Perry about the patent on his invention. He waited half an hour in the shop, and called out: "Mr. Perry, are you there? This is Eugene Smith!" But despite his calls he received no reply and deciding Perry must be occupied upstairs, possibly with another client, he left. The following day, September 4th, Smith returned again to the shop and found the place exactly as he had left it the previous day, and still no sign of Perry. He called out but once again received no answer, which surprised him. He decided to go upstairs to see if Perry was around, and in the back room of the house he found, lying in the glare of sunlight streaming through the window, the dead body of a man, whose face was burnt beyond recognition. He was lying with his feet towards the window and his head towards the door, and it seemed there had been some sort of explosion, for a broken bottle that had contained an inflammable liquid and a broken tobacco pipe, complete with burnt matches, were lying by the side of the body.

Not waiting any longer Smith ran from the building and called the Philadelphia Police whose officers arrived on the scene within minutes. They found that the general appearance of the dead man seemed to fit that of B.F. Perry, who was well known locally, and a later medical examination of the body showed that death was sudden and that there had been a paralysis of the involuntary muscles. The stomach of the dead man emitted a strong smell of chloroform and showed symptoms of alcohol irritation. An inquest that followed returned a verdict that B. F. Perry had died of congestion of the lungs caused by the inhalation of either flame or chloroform, and after eleven days in the morgue the body was buried.

Meanwhile the Fidelity Mutual Life Association's Philadelphia branch had received a letter from a St Louis attorney named Jephtha D. Howe, which stated that the dead man was actually Benjamin F. Pitezel of St Louis, and he was insured for ten thousand dollars. The letter said the insurance had been effected in November, 1893, and Howe said he intended coming to Philadelphia with some members of Pitezel's family in order to identify the remains. In referring to their Chicago branch the letter added that the only person who seemed to have known Pitezel when in that city was one H. H. Holmes who lived in Wilmette, Illinois. They contacted Holmes

Benjamin P. Pitezel

and forwarded a newspaper cutting to him which stated, wrongly, that B.F. Perry had died in Chicago.

On September 18th the insurance company received a letter from Holmes offering any help he could give in identifying B.F. Perry as B.F. Pitezel, and he gave the name of a Chicago dentist who, he claimed, would be able to recognise teeth he had made for Pitezel. In addition, Holmes gave a description of the dead man, with particular reference to a malformation on the knee and a wart on the back of his neck. He also offered, if his expenses were covered, to travel to Chicago to view the body, but two days later he wrote again saying he had read that the death had taken place in Philadelphia, not Chicago, but that, as he would be in Baltimore, a mere one hundred miles away, he would happily travel to Philadelphia and visit the office of the insurance company.

On September 20th, Holmes turned up at the office of the Fidelity Mutual Life Association in Philadelphia and once again offered help, and on learning that Jephtha D. Howe, the lawyer from St Louis, was due

A contemporary newspaper sketch of H.H. Holmes

to arrive in Philadelphia to represent the widow, Mrs Pitezel, and formally complete identification of the dead man, Holmes amiably agreed to return to the office and meet the attorney and offer any further help that was needed.

The following day Jephtha D. Howe did indeed arrive in Philadelphia accompanied by Alice Pitezel, the dead man's daughter, and he explained that Pitezel had taken the name of Perry owing to financial problems. The insurance company agreed that Perry and Pitezel were one and the same man, but for some reason were not convinced that the body belonged to Pitezel, and then mentioned Holmes' presence and offer of help with identification. Howe said he did not know anything about Holmes but he would be happy to meet him. By coincidence Holmes arrived at the office at that moment and he was introduced to Howe as a stranger, but was recognised as a friend by fifteen-year-old

Alice Pitezel

Alice, a shy girl. Formal greetings over, the group then arranged to meet again the following day in order to carry out the formality of identification on the corpse.

When the party met at Potter's Field Cemetery, where the body had been exhumed and laid out, the doctor on site said he was unable to find the distinguishing marks that would show that Perry and Pitezel were the same man, whereupon Holmes stepped forward, took off his coat, put on a pair of rubber gloves and taking a surgeon's knife from his pocket, cut off the wart at the back of the corpse's neck and showed the doctor the dead man's leg injury. The dead man was then covered over except for his mouth and Alice was brought forward and said the teeth appeared to be those of her father. The insurance company then declared themselves satisfied with the identification, and handed a cheque for $9,175 to Howe and ten dollars to H. H. Holmes for his travelling expenses.

Smith, the carpenter who had found the body in Callowhill Street, had also been present in Potter's Field, and for a moment he thought he detected in Holmes a likeness to the man he had seen in Perry's office on August 22nd and who had gone upstairs with him, but he was not confident enough to be certain, so he stayed silent.

Across in Missouri things were taking a different turn, for in St Louis Prison languished a man named Marion Hedgspeth who was serving twenty years for train robbery. On October 9th, 1894, he asked to see the prison governor and said he wanted to get in touch with the Fidelity Mutual Life Association as he had information to pass on to them. In his statement to the insurance company Hedgspeth said he had met, in prison the previous year, a man named H. M. Howard who was in jail on a fraud charge, but who was released on bail later the same month. While in prison Howard told Hedgspeth that he had thought of a plan for swindling an insurance company of $10,000 and promised Hedgspeth that if he would recommend a "good lawyer" for his purpose, Howard would share his fortune by giving Hedgspeth $500.

The thought of a pocket full of cash was a tempting offer and Howard had no hesitation in recommending Jephtha D. Howe who entered enthusiastically into the plan, telling Hedgspeth that he thought Howard "one of the smoothest and slickest" men he had known. The plan called for a corpse to be found which matched Pitezel's description which was to be treated as if it had been involved in a tragic accident. In the meantime, Pitezel himself was to disappear to Germany. Howe told Hedgspeth that the cover up had been successfully completed but had failed to deliver the promised $500, thus leaving the convict open to divulge the plot to the law enforcement authorities as way of revenge.

It soon became apparent that H. M. Howard and H. H. Holmes were one and the same person, and that Jephtha D. Howe and Holmes were not the strangers to each other that they had affected to be at their meeting in Philadelphia. The insurance company, while deciding to keep an open mind about the truth of Hedgspeth's statement, nevertheless called in the services of the highly successful and powerful Pinkerton National Detective Agency who set off on the track of H.H. Holmes, and only a month later they arrested him after tracking him to his father's home in Gilmanton, New Hampshire.

William A. Pinkerton, co-owner of the famous detective agency that helped track H.H. Holmes

The Pinkerton inquiries turned up evidence that early in 1894 Holmes and Pitezel had bought some property in Fort Worth, Texas, but soon left after authorities there became aware of several dubious transactions. There was also a case of suspected horse theft, on which Texas frowned so severely that they tended to hang those found guilty, so it is little wonder that the pair soon abandoned the lone star state and headed for the more genteel states of New England. While all the activity in Texas was going on, Pitezel had a wife, Carrie, and five children living in St Louis, though by the time Holmes and Pitezel left Texas she and two of the children were then living in Burlington, Vermont, and she was arrested and charged with complicity in the insurance fraud and was taken to Boston.

Two days after Holmes was arrested he made a statement to police in which he freely acknowledged the fraud, and said the body that had been substituted for Pitezel had been obtained from a New York doctor. It had, Holmes said, been packed in a trunk and shipped to Philadelphia. At this stage he declined to name the doctor. He openly admitted that Pitezel had gone with three of his children to South America, though Holmes had not bothered to mention this fact to Mrs Pitezel who, by the time she had arrived in Boston, was greatly distressed and bewildered by events beyond her control.

She was questioned by detectives but denied any conspiracy in the fraud, though she was more concerned for news of what had happened to her husband and children. She had not seen her daughter Alice since she had travelled to Philadelphia to identify what she thought were her father's remains. She told the officers that shortly afterwards Holmes had gone to St Louis and taken away her children Nellie and Howard supposedly to join Alice who he had said was living with a widow in Ovington, Kentucky.

Nellie Pitezel

"Since that day, I haven't seen any of the children, or my husband," Carrie Pitezel cried. "I was advised by Mr. Holmes to go to Detroit, then Toronto, and on to Ogdensberg and, lastly, to Burlington in the hope of seeing my husband and children, but I haven't seen any of them. I believe my husband has deserted me and taken the children with him!" she said.

On November 20th, Holmes and Carrie were taken from Boston to Philadelphia where, with Benjamin

Howard Pitezel

Pitezel and Jephtha D. Howe, they were charged with defrauding the Fidelity Life Association of $10,000. After being charged Holmes was asked by an insurance investigator who had helped pack the body in the trunk sent from New York to Philadelphia and Holmes, always keen to be the centre of attention, said he had done it alone having learnt the 'trick' while studying medicine in Michigan. The investigator pointed out that when the body had been removed from Callowhill Street it had been rigid and straight.

He asked: "What trick did you learn in medical school by which it was possible to re-stiffen a body after the rigor mortis has been broken?" Holmes remained silent, but he realised he had made a big mistake. A couple of weeks later he volunteered to make a second statement and in a complete turnaround now said that Pitezel, in a state of depression following a drinking bout, had committed suicide in the property in Callowhill Street. Holmes added that having found the body he had carried it downstairs and arranged it in a manner designed to fool the insurance company into thinking a terrible accident had happened. Holmes explained that Pitezel had killed himself by lying on the floor and inhaled chloroform through a tube into his mouth. He added that Pitezel's three missing children had gone to England to stay with a woman friend of his called Minnie Williams.

Minnie Williams was the woman from whom Holmes claimed he had bought the land in Fort Worth, and there was also a tragedy, he said, about the life of Miss Williams who had first come to him in 1893 as secretary of a drug store he was then running in Chicago. They soon became intimate and later in the same year wrote to her sister Nannie saying she was getting married to a handsome, wealthy and eloquent man by the name of Harry Gordon (alias Holmes) and invited her to attend. Nannie turned up but before long a serious row broke out between the sisters and, Holmes added, he came home to find that Minnie had killed Nannie in a fit of temper and he had disposed of the body by dumping her in Chicago's Lake Michigan.

By this time, claimed Holmes, he and Minnie had married, but she was so distraught about the death of her sister that it was an easy task to persuade her to travel to England with Pitezel's three children and start a new life until he could join them at sometime in the future. What Minnie did not know at this time was that Holmes also had three other 'wives' all ignorant of each other.

Detectives did not believe any of this and suspected that Holmes, real name Herman W. Mudgett, then aged thirty-four, was covering up his tracks and suspected him of murdering Pitezel and the three missing children. Their extensive inquiries revealed that Holmes had spent his early days in Vermont as a farmer's boy before taking up medicine and obtaining a medical degree. They also discovered that Holmes and a fellow student, finding a body that bore a singular resemblance to the latter, carried out a fraud on an insurance company and obtained

Herman W. Mudgett

$1,000. The scheme they had used was almost identical to the attempt to defraud the Fidelity Mutual Life Association in Philadelphia. After spending some time working for an asylum in Pennsylvania, Holmes set off for Chicago and set up shop as a druggist and was so successful that he was soon building a huge four storey property on the corner of Wallace and 63rd Street which later became known as 'Holmes Castle'.

The building was unique. The lower section was offices and a shop, while Holmes occupied the second floor and had a laboratory on the third floor. Within his office was an air-proof and sound-proof vault, while in the bathroom was a trapdoor, covered with a rug, which opened onto a secret staircase which connected his laboratory to the cellar. In the cellar was a large grate.

Holmes' notorious 'Castle' in Chicago

It was to 'Holmes Castle' that Minnie Williams had invited Nannie and it was here where Holmes claimed the tragedy of Nannie's death took place. Minnie would undoubtedly have looked differently on the heavy moustachioed Holmes had she only known about his other 'wives' and his life was such a web of deceit that it took detectives some time to unravel. He had first married, under his real name, in 1878, and was actually visiting his first wife in Vermont when Pinkerton's men first set off on his trail. The second 'marriage' took place in Chicago under the alias Howard, and the third in Denver, Colorado, in January, 1894, under the name H. H. Holmes, and this 'wife' had been with him when he arrived in Philadelphia to identify Pitezel's body.

By the start of 1895 Holmes was still in jail in Philadelphia, and though the authorities knew they had him in the frame for the fraud charge, they wanted to know what had happened to the Pitezel children, Alice, Nellie and Howard. District Attorney George S. Graham called for

Holmes to be brought to his office where he questioned him.

"It is strongly suspected, Holmes, that you have not only murdered Pitezel, but that you have killed the children. The best way to remove this suspicion is to produce the children at once. Now, where are they? Tell me and I will use every means in my power to secure their early recovery... I am almost persuaded that your word cannot be depended upon, yet I am not averse to giving you an opportunity to assist me in clearing up the mystery which surrounds their disappearance and their present abode, and I ask you to answer frankly and truthfully. Where are the children?"

Holmes pursed his lips and answered in a calm voice: "The last time I saw Howard was in Detroit, Michigan. There I gave him to Miss Williams (Minnie) who took him to Buffalo, New York, from which point she proceeded to Niagara Falls. After the departure of Howard I took Alice and Nellie to Toronto, Canada, where they remained for several days. At Toronto I purchased railroad tickets for them for Niagara Falls, put them on the train, and rode out of Toronto with them a few miles, so that they would be assured that they were on the right train. Before their departure, I prepared a telegram which they should send me from the Falls, if they failed to meet Miss Williams and Howard, and I also carefully pinned in the dress of Alice, four hundred dollars in large bills, so Miss Williams would be in funds to defray their expenses."

He added that the girls had met their brother and Minnie at Niagara Falls from which point they continued their journey to New York City where Minnie dressed Nellie as a boy and took a steamer for Liverpool and onwards to London.

"If you search among the steamship offices in New York, you must search for a woman and a girl and two boys, and not a woman and two girls and a boy. This was all done to throw the detectives off the track, who were after me for the insurance fraud. Miss Williams opened a massage establishment at 80 Veder or Vadar Street, London. I have no doubt the children are with her now, and very likely at that place." A tearful Holmes added: "Why should I kill innocent children?"

When he was asked to give the name of anyone who had seen Williams with the children he resented the questioning of his truthfulness and suggested that a cypher advertisement be placed in the New York Herald, by which means he claimed to have agreed to correspond with Minnie Williams. The advertisement was placed in the paper but produced no reply, and inquiries from Scotland Yard officers in London produced the not unexpected news that no such address as Veder or Vadar Street existed in London.

By this time Mrs Pitezel had been released from custody and the fraud conspiracy charge against her had been dropped, and she was still totally distraught at the disappearance of her children. Holmes wrote to her and said: "Knowing me as you do, can you imagine me killing little and innocent children, especially without any motive?" But the letter did nothing to appease Mrs Pitezel who recalled that just before his arrest Holmes had taken her to a house he had rented in Burlington, Vermont, and how one day he had asked her to carry a package of nitroglycerine from the bottom to the top of the house, and how she had once discovered him removing boards in the cellar.

The children had disappeared in October 1894 and by this time, June 1895, the trail looked like getting cold, but one man who was determined that every possible lead be followed no matter how long it took was Philadelphia detective Frank Geyer, a man with a reputation for his doggedness. He started his search by travelling to Cincinnati with photographs of the entire Pitezel family and pictures of three trunks that had also gone missing. Once in Cincinnati Geyer called on an old friend, detective John Schnooks to assist him and the pair first started checking hotel registers around rail depots and eventually came across a cheap hotel called Atlantic House where the clerk produced a September 28th registration entry for an Alexander E. Cook and three children. The inquiries then turned to estate agents as Holmes was known to regularly rent houses in whichever town he stayed in for any length of time, and this line produced dividends when they found that Holmes had indeed rented a house at 305 Poplar Street under the name of A.C. Hayes, and paid fifteen dollars in advance.

Detective Frank Geyer

Talking to the neighbour next door to number 305, the detectives were told that on September 29th a man had arrived at the house in a furniture wagon with a boy, and the neighbour had been astonished to realise that the only furniture taken into the house was a large iron cylinder stove. The neighbour added that she had been even more astonished the following day when Mr Hayes told her he had changed his mind about living there and made her a present of the stove.

The trail took Geyer to Indianapolis where he enlisted the help of detective David Richards and their inquiries found that on September 30th, the same day 'Hayes' had changed his mind, a man with three children had arrived at the Hotel English and registered in the name of Canning, Mrs Pitezel's maiden name. The man was identified from a photograph as Holmes, and Gayer must have been jubilant that he was on the right trail. Unfortunately they only stayed one night and the trail looked as though it would fade again until he was reminded by Richards of another hotel called the Circle House which had since closed. They managed to find the hotel registers after some difficulty and discovered that the three Canning children had indeed arrived on October 1st and stayed until the 10th. The former owner of the hotel, Herman Ackelow, told them that Holmes had described himself as the children's uncle and had said that Howard was a "bad child" whom he intended placing in an institution. He added that the children were seldom let out of the room and they often cried and were unhappy and obviously homesick.

Thanking detective Richards for his assistance, Geyer followed the trail to Detroit where he discovered that two girls known as "Etta and Nellie Canning" had arrived on October 12th and had been registered at the New Western Hotel where they stayed for three days before moving to a local boarding house in Congress Street. From Detroit Alice had written to her grandparents that it was cold and wet and she and Etta had bad colds and chapped hands. "We have to stay in all the time. All that Nell and I can do is to draw...I wish I could see you all. I am getting so homesick that I don't know what to do."

Ironically, Alice's mother was at that moment less than a five minutes walk from her. She had arrived in the city on October 14th with her other two children Dessie and baby Wharton, and took a room at Geis's Hotel, in the name of Mrs Adams. She appeared to be in distress and stayed constantly in her room. At the same time there had been staying at another Detroit hotel, a couple registered as Mr and Mrs Holmes, this being Holmes and his third 'wife'. The three parties, Alice and Nellie, Mrs Pitezel and her two younger children, and the third Mrs Holmes, were all ignorant of each other's presence and it was only Holmes himself who was able to balance their lives. It was under his secret guidance too that all three parties left Detroit, crossing into Canada and arriving in Toronto on October 18th and again registering in three different hotels! The only one of the parties which did not appear to be anywhere in Toronto was the "bad" child Howard, whom detective Geyer soon suspected of having been murdered – but where was his body if that was indeed the case?

Geyer's inquiries revealed that "Alice and Nellie Canning" had stayed at the Albion Hotel in Toronto, having arrived there on October 19th and left on October 25th. During their stay a man, identified by hotel staff as Holmes, had called each morning for the two children and taken them out with him, though they always returned alone in time for supper. But on October 25th, Holmes had called for the children and taken them out, but they failed to return.

More inquiries by Geyer, aided by an appeal in the press, revealed that a man answering Holmes's description had rented a house at 16 St Vincent Street in the previous October and that he had been accompanied by two young girls but no boy. Holmes told his next door neighbour, an elderly Scottish man named Thomas Ryves, that he had taken the house for his widowed sister but the only furniture taken into the house had been a bed, a mattress and a trunk. Holmes also borrowed a spade off Ryves telling him he wanted to dig a place in the cellar where his sister could keep potatoes, and had returned the tool the following day.

All this information was told to detective Geyer and it didn't take long for him to have Holmes recognised as the man who had rented the house by showing his photograph to Frank Nudel who owned the property. Convinced more than ever that he was now dealing with multiple murder, the detective hastened to St Vincent Street and borrowed off Ryves the very spade he had loaned Holmes and, after getting permission from the present occupant of number 16, he began to make a search of the small, dark cellar, in the company of detective Alf Cuddy, another old friend who worked for the Toronto Police.

Geyer later wrote: "Taking the spade and pushing it into the earth, so as to determine whether it had been lately dug up, we finally discovered a soft spot in the southwest corner. Forcing the spade into the earth, we found it easy digging, and after going about one foot, a horrible stench arose. This convinced us that we were on the right spot, and our coats were thrown off, and with renewed confidence, we continued our digging. The deeper we dug, the more horrible the odour became, and when we reached the depth of three feet, we discovered what appeared to be the bone of the forearm of a human being."

Further examination found the remains of two children in an advanced state of decomposition, and these were later identified as the bodies of Alice and Nellie by their mother, who was only able to identify them by their hair and teeth. Corroborative evidence of their identification came from questioning the occupant who had taken the house after Holmes. Geyer learnt that a little toy wooden egg with a snake in it which belonged to the Pitezel youngsters had been found by the incoming tenant, while a later tenant had found some clothing stuffed up the chimney which answered the description of clothing belonging to the children.

The problem remained for Geyer – what had happened to young Howard? The detective had so far established that Holmes had rented houses in Cincinnati, Detroit and Toronto and that Howard had been seen with his sisters in Indianapolis while in Detroit house agents seemed vague about a boy being with Holmes. Geyer returned to Detroit to continue his inquiries and further questioning of the estate agents, and an exhaustive search of the house Holmes had rented in that city, convinced the Philadelphia detective that the boy had never been in Detroit and seemed to have disappeared in Indianapolis. Thus Geyer moved on to Indianapolis to continue his investigation.

Meanwhile, back in Philadelphia, Holmes had the newspapers delivered to him in his prison cell and he learnt about the discovery of the children's bodies in Toronto. In his journal Holmes wrote: "On the morning of the 16th of July, my newspaper was delivered to me about 8.30am, and I had hardly opened it before I saw in large headlines the announcement of the finding of the children in Toronto. For the moment it seemed so impossible that I was inclined to think it was one of the frequent newspaper excitements that had attended the earlier part of the case, but, in attempting to gain some accurate comprehension of what was stated in the article, I became convinced that at least certain bodies had been found there, and upon comparing the date when the house was hired I knew it to be the same as when the children had been in Toronto; and thus being forced to realise the awfulness of what had probably happened, I gave up trying to read the article, and saw instead the two little faces as they had looked when I hurriedly left them – felt the innocent child's kiss so timidly given, and heard again their earnest words of farewell, and realised that I had received another burden to carry to my grave with me, equal, if not worse, than the horrors of Nannie Williams' death."

Detective Geyer continued his search in Indianapolis by obtaining a list of advertisements for houses let in the area during 1894, and he painstakingly followed up nine hundred of them without success. When he turned his attention to small towns he found the task just as daunting and wrote to his bosses in Philadelphia: "By Monday we will have searched every outlying town except Irvington. After Irvington, I scarcely know where we shall go." Two months had passed since the search begun, and on August 17th he entered Irvington where he immediately spotted the office of an estate agent. In a pattern which he had repeated hundreds of times Geyer opened his photographs and asked the agent if he recognised the portrait of Holmes.

The response was immediate: "Yes, I remember him," the agent said. He went on to say that he had given the keys to a nearby cottage to Holmes in October 1894 and recalled him clearly for he had been abrupt and rude, and added "I felt that he should have had more respect for my grey hairs!"

From the estate agent's office Geyer headed for the cottage and made at once for the cellar but could find no sign of any disturbance. But under the floor of a piazza adjoining the cottage he found the remains of a trunk which answered the description of one the Pitezel children had with them, and in an outhouse he discovered a stove with bloodstains on the top. A further search revealed in the cellar chimney some bones, a pelvis, teeth, and the baked remains of a liver, stomach and spleen which a medical examination later revealed were those of a child between seven and ten years old. More inquiries found that a pair of shoes, a scarf pin, a spinning top and several articles of clothing had been found in the house at different times and these were handed to

Geyer who had them identified as belonging to the Pitezel children.

On September 1st, exhausted but jubilant, Geyer returned to Philadelphia in time for Holmes' trial for the murder of Benjamin Pitezel that started on October 28th, 1895. During the trial District Attorney George S. Graham offered to put in evidence showing that Holmes had murdered the three Pitezel children on the grounds that such evidence was admissible because the murder of the children and their father were all part of the same transaction, but the judge refused the offer. Holmes' defence did not contest the identity of Pitezel's body found in Callowhill Street, though they maintained the old argument offered by their client that Pitezel had committed suicide. His plea of not guilty to murder was shallow enough for the jury to find Holmes guilty of killing Pitezel and on November 2nd, H.H. Holmes was sentenced to death.

Holmes gassing the children

If the result of the murder trial had gone in Holmes' favour, the Philadelphia Police and other police departments were waiting in the wings ready to pounce on him again, for they had carried out an exhaustive search of 'Holmes Castle' in Chicago, and in the stove in the cellar detectives had found charred human bones, while in the centre of the room was a large dissecting table stained with blood. In the cellar floor they found more human bones, including vertebrae, ribs and teeth, and in other parts of the infamous building they found more charred bones, metal buttons, a trunk and watch chain which was identified as once belonging to Minnie Williams.

A month before he was due to be executed, following failed appeals to the courts, Holmes sold his story for $7,500 to newspapers. Confessing to twenty-seven murders, though the day after the story was published he claimed the confession was a fake. He said he was tired of being accused in the press of every murder that had taken place during the previous ten years so he had decided to give the newspapers a sensational story!

The true number of victims who met their end at the hands of H.H. Holmes may never be known, but it has been estimated that at least ten met their death in the Chicago 'castle'. What is certain is that had Holmes not made the mistake of confiding in Hedgspeth his plan for defrauding the Philadelphia insurance company, or if he had at least kept his part of the bargain and handed the crook his promised $500, the evil career of this mass killer may not have come to light until his tally of victims reached unthinkable numbers.

H.H. Holmes was executed in Philadelphia's Moyamensing Prison on May 7th, 1896, but even in death this notorious criminal would not go quietly, for he had given instructions to his lawyer that his body was to be encased in cement and buried ten feet deep before his coffin too was covered with still more cement. This singular wish, designed to stop body-snatchers or his corpse being sold (an offer of $5,000 had been made to his lawyer Samuel P. Rotan the day before his execution) was carried out to the letter by Philadelphia prison and police officials and Herman W. Mudgett, alias H.H. Holmes, was buried in Holy Cross Cemetery, Delamere County, and his death certificate gave his cause of death as "hanging according to law."

THE WILL MAKER
The case of Richard Brinkley

LAURA Jane Glen left her home in one of Warwickshire's many mining villages in the autumn of 1892. Seeking new luck and a chance to break away from her working class background, the seventeen-year-old set off for London where she met widower William Ridgley. Thirty-seven-year-old Ridgley had been widowed some nine years and of his many children, only one, Richard, was living with him at his Chelsea home. After a short time Laura Glen committed suicide and Ridgley found himself appearing before a coroner's court. His evidence was open to question – he denied that they slept together when it was pretty clear that they did, she had died from arsenic poisoning yet he explained away his stash of arsenic and prussic acids as having been used for his 'experiments' and he claimed Laura and he were not lovers. Although Ridgley was not under suspicion for murder, the court recorded their unhappiness at the quantities of poison under his control.

Our story moves to Croydon in 1906. One Richard Brinkley had befriended a retired maternity nurse in her late seventies. Joanna Blume shared her large house with her struggling actress granddaughter, Augusta. Brinkley was a regular visitor to the house offering the old lady advice on her investments and on family matters. He was humorous, intelligent, a good listener, and a member of the local Masonic Lodge.

On December 19th Augusta, who was rehearsing at the Palace Theatre in Fulham received an urgent message to return home. Joanna Blume had been found dead from natural causes, lying on the living room floor. That evening both Brinkley and Augusta's aunt Caroline attended the house to offer their individual condolences during which Caroline announced that as next of kin, she intended to claim her new house. She must have been dumb-founded when Brinkley revealed the existence of a will, made two days earlier, leaving everything to him. This document was presented to solicitors who declared it valid.

Augusta saw nothing wrong in Brinkley's inheritance – he had been a good friend to her grandmother and anyway, Caroline and Joanna hadn't seen eye to eye for many years. Caroline however, wasn't so easily assured and she took her concerns to another solicitor who lodged a caveat against the will. This required Brinkley to produce two witnesses to swear that they had been present when Joanna Blume had signed the will. Builder Henry Heard and accountant Reginald Parker had indeed witnessed the document – although this fact didn't stop Brinkley from panicking. He went to see Caroline offering to sell the house and split the proceeds with her but to no avail, then he offered to marry her saying it had been Joanna's last request to him – she declined. Finally, he offered her a more lucrative financial deal but no, she was set on a court room battle.

Richard Brinkley had a secret – not only was his real name William Ridgley, but he had indeed tricked Joanna Blume into signing the will he had had prepared for her. Ridgley had many skills but writing wasn't one of them so he had sought and gained the help of part-time accountant and part-time livestock keeper Reginald Parker. Ridgley had come across Parker because they shared a love of keeping poultry – although in truth, Ridgley experimented on his chickens using poisons - and because both had suffered failed marriages. Parker was in some heavy financial difficulties and Ridgley had offered to set up a fraudulent bankruptcy scheme to shake off his debtors. Parker witnessed the will although he claimed later that Ridgley had duped him into signing it. The second witness was Henry Heard, a builder who had visited the Blume house ostensibly to repair a ceiling but who had in fact, written the will and witnessed it. Ridgley knew that if Caroline's suspicions could be proved both he and Heard would risk jail. The only person who could tell on them was Reg Parker.

Parker called on 'Brinkley' in his newly inherited house one evening and settled down for a drinking session. 'Brinkley' was a tee-totaller and so Parker found himself the only one with a glass of whiskey. For some reason, never properly explained, Parker suspected 'Brinkley' might be trying to poison him and threw the whiskey in the fire. He was right to be wary, 'Brinkley' was indeed trying to kill him. Some weeks later he visited Parker taking with him a bottle of poisoned liquor but as Parker had company the plan couldn't be carried out. Parker then moved into new lodgings, sharing a house with a couple called Beck and their two children. The Becks had agreed that Parker could entertain a friend at their home on the evening of Saturday 20th April. 'Brinkley' arrived by train, calling at an off licence on the way to buy a bottle of beer to take with him. 'Brinkley' poured a glass each and then asked Parker to fetch him a glass of water. When he was out of the room 'Brinkley' added prussic acid to the brew but when Parker returned he suggested the two men take a walk to discuss 'Brinkley' buying Parker's bulldog. The glasses were left untouched.

Parker bade 'Brinkley' farewell at the tram stop and returned to his digs. The Becks had now returned from their day out and Mr Beck helped himself to a glass of beer, offering his wife a sip. With the glasses now almost empty, the adults went to the kitchen leaving one child, Daisy, in the room. Tragically, the child tasted the beer and within minutes Richard and Elizabeth Beck were dead and Daisy was fighting for her life. Parker returned to discover the bodies, the police were called and Daisy, finally, recovered - only to discover she and her sister Hilda, were orphans.

The following day the police arrived at Ridgley's house.
"We are police officers," said Detective Inspector Henry Fowler, "and I shall arrest you for administering poison in a bottle of stout to Reginald Parker at Croydon last night, with intent to murder him."
"Well, I'm buggered!" replied Ridgley.

It was soon after that the police revealed the deaths of Mr and Mrs Beck for whose murders Ridgley would most likely also be charged. Later he claimed not to have seen Parker for three weeks and that this was probably one of Parker's practical jokes. The following morning Ridgley asked the police whether Parker had told them that he was guilty and he also confided that he was a tee-totaller and therefore did not buy beer. No one had accused him of purchasing the stout and his comments aroused suspicion so much so that the police set about discovering where the bottle had indeed been acquired. It was a fatal mistake as John Holden, the boy who had served Ridgley came forward to help the police with their enquiries. The boy recalled Ridgley, two evenings earlier, coming into the off licence on Brighton Road. He had asked for a bottle of oatmeal stout and had complained at having to pay the 2d deposit. He left only to return ten minutes later to pay up. Holden could identify him.

The coroner found that the Becks had died from prussic poisoning which led to enquiries into Ridgley's associates. The police uncovered a friendship with a William Vale, an expert in ornithology and the diseases affecting birds. 'Brinkley' had been a regular visitor to Vale's workshop and had been left alone with large supplies of poisons – and Vale suspected he had been stealing them. Vale, Daisy and Hilda Beck and Reginald Parker were all called to give evidence. Parker proved a damning witness, revealing details of 'Brinkley's' attempts to poison him, of his attempts to persuade him to write a will and of his threats. It was this evidence that decided the police on their next step – to exhume the body of Joanna Blume.

The coroner could find no evidence that Joanna Blume had met an untimely death – and who knows, maybe she did die from natural causes. Her grandaughter though, set about undermining 'Brinkley' in the press and other witnesses spoke of seeing the old lady's possessions in pawnshops within days of her funeral. Caroline was forced to come clean about her living arrangements and revealed the existence of several children, a disabled husband and mounting debts. Could she have cooked up the whole challenge to the will simply for much needed personal gain?

On May 28th 1906 'Brinkley' made his last appearance in court to hear Reginald Parker's ex-wife tell the court that Parker had forged a will for 'Brinkley's' own grandmother and been promised "a hundred" if all went well. There was also talk of a black wig 'Brinkley' had sometimes worn and evidence that he often dyed his moustache. It was put to the court that here was a very odd fellow indeed and a trial date was set.

Henry Heard was called to give evidence at the coroners court where he was asked to explain how he came to witness Joanna Blume's will. Heard, although sticking to his tale that he had been working at the house when Blume had asked for his signature, admitted to having known 'Brinkley' for two years. Heard in fact stumbled through five hours of questioning and in the end, the coroner stated for the record that he hadn't believed a word of his evidence. The jury decided that 'Brinkley' had a case to answer and for the second time that week he was sent for trial.

On July 22nd 1907 the trial began. Over the next two days our colourful cast of characters reiterated their evidence and notably, for the first time, testimony was allowed regarding the ink used in the writing of the will. On the third day 'Brinkley' took the stand and amongst his many denials was one that he had never bought a bottle of stout nor had he visited the Beck household. His alibi was that he had been enjoying the company of a shopkeeper friend, a Mr Snapper. The boy Holden was produced, as was an Inspector who had chatted to him as he waited for the Croydon train – but no, 'Brinkley' had been with Mr Snapper. In the end, he was challenged to produce this witness.

The following day, the judge asked whether Mr Snapper had come to court. He had not. Following the summing up, the jury retired to deliberate on its verdict. Within the hour they were back and the judge, Mr Justice Bigham, was placing the black cap on his head.

The prosecution had failed to call one of its witnesses. Sergeant Overton's evidence was in regard of the suicide of Laura Jane Glen, some fourteen years earlier. In just under a fortnight 'Brinkley', or 'Ridgley' was hung. He denied his son a last visit and he took many secrets with him to the grave – did he kill Laura, Joanna, his grandmother and his first wife? We shall never know but just after the trial finished a former landlady sold a story to the press. She spoke of 'Brinkley' returning home one night and asking whether he could light a fire in his room. She agreed little knowing that he was planning arson. Luckily for the residents, a quick-thinking tenant returning home in the middle of the night managed to put the blaze out. As she told the reporters, "There were eight people in that house – we could have burnt to death in our beds!". 'Brinkley' it turned out, had insured the contents of his room and made thirteen pounds from the fire.

Gift of the Gab!

The phrase 'the gift of the gab' could have been invented for the wonderfully named Horatio Bottomley. Larger than life and twice as colourful, Bottomley started his career as a small-time court reporter soon moving into the more lucrative world of publishing. By 1891 however, he was bankrupt and amid a swirl of ever more furious debtors, details of alleged fraud began to surface. The erudite Bottomley talked himself out of trouble and into another venture.

Horatio Bottomley

This time it was mining - he sold stock in Australian gold. All in all his portfolio totalled over £20 million spread across some 50 companies. Each one eventually went under with investors losing their shirts - all except Bottomley who made £3 million out of the sorry mess. In 1906 he launched a newspaper, the *John Bull*, and stood successfully for parliament. Both these developments afforded him a public voice and he lost no time at all in denouncing anyone who questioned his past. His career in the 'house' was short-lived however and in 1912 he declared himself bankrupt once more which forced him to relinquish his seat.

Bottomley soon bounced back and by now was living the high life with a racing stable, a London home, a country pile and a lavish villa in the South of France - all registered in his wife's name. He now embarked on a fraud involving the running of a lottery - he pocketed as much money as he could, fixed the draws and stole the winnings. Incredibly he was re-elected to parliament after the First World War and he soon used his position to run another racket - Victory War Bonds from which he amassed further large sums.

Not before time, in 1922 Horatio Bottomley was sent to prison where he served five years for his frauds. His wife died in 1930 and he followed three years later, destitute and living off the charity of one of his many mistresses. A colourful character indeed!

AN IMAGINATION FOR THE TRUTH
The strange affair of the two Mr Druces!

THE Druce-Portand case caused a sensation in its day with over 96 articles penned on it between 1907 and 1909 in The Times newspaper alone! Two families were involved, the nouveau riche Druces and the old money of the Cavendish-Bentinck's...

On land leased from the Portman estate, a builder named William Baker laid out Baker Street from 1755 onwards. This London thoroughfare was lined with residential and retail properties. In 1822 Druce and Company, owned by 27-year-old Thomas Charles Druce, opened a furniture business within a retail development known as 'The Baker Street Bazaar' at numbers 58 and 59.

The enterprise appears to have flourished, as did the 'Bazaar', which housed such attractions as 'The London Glacarium' and 'Tussauds'. The Druce family prospered and Thomas and his wife Annie became parents – to Herbert (b. 1847) and Walter (b. 1852). By this time they were residing in a large country residence, Holcombe House, in Mill Hill. In September 1864 Thomas fell ill suffering with abscesses of the stomach and on December 19th gangrene set in. On December 28th he died in his bed at Holcombe House in his 71st year. His son Herbert, who claimed, to have been present at the time of death, registered his demise the following morning at Hendon.

The new widow, Annie, purchased a 20-guinea plot at the lavish Highgate Cemetery. Here, near the majestic Egyptian Avenue, in square 20, plans were made for the building of a brick vault 9 feet by 6 feet by 10 feet deep. In order that a burial service could take place prior to the completion of building work, Annie purchased for £10.10s a shelf in the public catacombs and so it was here that Druce's lead lined coffin was originally laid to rest. Some months later, and the casket was moved, at a cost of £2.2s., to the newly constructed vault. A tall stone monument featuring scrolls and wreaths topped by three steps and a draped urn was erected in simple remembrance of Thomas. A simple inscription read, *"Sacred to the memory of Thomas Charles Druce of Mill Hill, Hendon. Who departed this life December 28th 1864 in his 71st year."*

Madame Tussaud's second home on Marylebone Road

The family, as was then common, withdrew from society in order to hide their grief, but they continued to control the Baker Street store. In 1868 Louie, Herbert's wife, gave birth to Thomas' first grandson, Hamilton. A new generation had begun. But our tale now focuses on another family

On September 17th 1800 William John Cavendish-Scott-Bentinck, second son of William and Henrietta, was born. This was no ordinary family though; William's father was the Duke of Portland. Educated at home, one of nine children, the young William was prone to ill health. Indeed, his short-lived army career was dogged by bouts of lethargy.

In 1824, his elder brother died and William became Marquis of Titchfield and MP for Kings Lynn. The family traditionally held the parliamentary seat and indeed, two years later William passed it on to his younger brother George. William travelled across Europe, again suffering illness, this time short-term memory loss and sciatica. In 1850 he was almost killed when a cab knocked him down! In 1854 his father passed away and William became 5th Duke of Portland a title he held until his death in 1879.

William is best remembered for his eccentricities. Although clearly a kind and gentle man, a lover of horses and hunting, a devotee of opera, a tireless charity worker, William spent much of his time and money developing the family estate, Welbeck Abbey, and his London home, Portland House. Here he erected ground glass screens 80 feet high and 200 feet long on either side of the gardens to ensure privacy whereas at Welbeck, subterranean carriage-ways, a riding house lit by 7,500 gas-lights, an enormous underground ballroom and stabling for over 96 horses were some of the more outlandish additions. Obsessed with anonymity, the Duke wore top hats two feet tall, heavy long overcoats even in summer, trousers tied at the knees and was often shielded by umbrellas. He travelled in shuttered coaches and when journeying between his homes, his wagonette would be loaded on board a train – the Duke never publicly stepping from it. On July 1st 1879 he made his last trip to London where he died, unmarried, childless and the last male of the line. He was buried at the General Cemetery Company's 'All Souls Cemetery' in London's Kensal Green.

William Cavendish Bentinck in bronze

By this time Welbeck was in a poor state with many rooms unusable, several completely bare and any number stuffed with boxes of Balbriggan socks, each embroidered with a coronet and the initials WA for Welbeck Abbey. The newspapers of the day widely reported details of the Duke's eccentric life – were these tabloid details what initially sparked an idea in the Druce family's minds?

In 1896, some 17 years after the Duke's death, Anna Maria Druce, widow of Walter, Thomas' younger son who had died back in 1880 aged 28, wrote an extraordinary letter to the then Home Secretary. She claimed that as if to crown the Duke's eccentric lifestyle, he had invented the character of Thomas Charles Druce and had been leading a double life.

The Duke's sister, Lucy, Countess Howard de Walden, was horrified.

Her brother's wealth had now passed to her and she wasn't giving it over to anyone! News of the claim spread and the tabloids had a field day – accounts of a tunnel connecting Portland House with the Baker Street Bazaar began to spread, there were photographs of the two men to show the likeness and even claims that the Duke wore false whiskers when pretending to be Druce. Suddenly the family was famous but not everyone believed Anna Maria and trouble soon courted her. In 1899 she was bound over for assaulting a Mrs Bentley, who doubted the claim. By 1903 the strain took its toll and Anna Maria was retired to an asylum, the same year that Portland House was demolished. The rest of the family, Herbert and Louie, their children Hamilton and Daisy, declined to take up the claim – but why? Well, one reason is that Herbert had registered his father's death, if the claim were true then Herbert had lied and therefore committed an offence. Another possibility is that Herbert duped the family doctor – oddly there is no record of a doctor seeing the body – and was therefore hiding his part in the deception. Either way, it was left to another of Thomas' grandsons, George Hollamby Druce, to return home from Australia and carry on the fight, in fact, into the courts.

To provide a fighting fund, the family established a public limited company, "The Druce-Portland Company Limited", selling shares at five shillings each, to be cashed in once the family had made its millions, for £16 each. George raised £25,000 in this way – a huge testament to the public's faith in the story.

In November 1907, 11 years after Mrs Druce had astounded the public with her claims, the case came to court. In fact, two cases were begun, the first was to establish the claim that the two men were one and the same and the other was a case brought by George against Herbert for falsifying his declaration that he witnessed Thomas' death.

On November 1st George's counsel called an elderly witness, a Miss Robinson. She claimed to have known the Duke when she was a slip of a girl and she had journeyed from New Zealand to give her evidence. She brought with her, as evidence, a diary, which she told the court she had deposited on arrival in London at Messrs Oswald Hanson and Smith, her solicitors. She borrowed the book from their safe and when returning it, it had been stolen from her as she was looking in a shop window, by a man who had distracted her by telling her there was a spider on her shoulder! This incident had been reported to Scotland Yard. Miss Robinson also explained to the court that several key letters, which were to have served as evidence, had been stolen from her luggage on the ship from New Zealand.

On November 8th Herbert appeared in court before Mr Justice Plowden to answer the summons that he, "Had committed perjury in the affidavit sworn by him at The Beeches, Circus Road, Saint Johns Wood on April 28th 1898 and in the probate court on December 3rd and 4th 1901." Mr Horace Avory KC, Sir Charles Matthews and Ronald Walker defended him; Mr Atherley-Jones QC and Mr Goodman led the prosecution. Mr Rowlatt watched on behalf of the Portlands, Mr Crispe KC and Mr Swanton for shareholders of 'Druce-Portland Limited' and the galleries were full of what the newspapers described as, "intrigued ladies"!

The affidavit had read, "I am the son of Thomas Charles Druce and was born July 4th 1846. I lived with my father from my birth until the time of his death. My father went to reside at Holcombe House, Mill Hill, Hendon, some three or four years before the year 1864, when he died. About the month of September 1864, my father fell ill, and he generally became worse, and died on December 28th 1864, between one and two in the morning. On December 28th I saw my father lying in his coffin. He was wrapped in a sheet and only his head was to be seen. I attended the funeral of my father along with Mr Alexander Young, Dr Shaw and many others. The burial took place at Highgate Cemetery and I saw the coffin laid in the catacombs there, from whence it was afterwards removed to the vault where it now lies."

This statement threw up another question – on Thomas' death certificate Herbert is listed as being present at the time of death however, the affidavit indicates otherwise, that Herbert merely saw the body lying in state. To George's team this didn't really matter, just seeing the body was enough. To them, of course, there hadn't been one.

The prosecution called Robert Caldwell of Richmond, Virginia. This seventy-one-year old, an Irishman by birth, claimed to have been introduced to the Duke by a friend. He had visited him both in London and at Welbeck and he had treated him for "malady". Caldwell had been given the task of organising the mock funeral for Druce. He had ordered a £50 coffin on 27th December, the day before the alleged death, he had purchased 200lb of sheet lead with which to fill the casket and he had assisted the Duke in screwing the lid down.

Caldwell identified photographs of the 'two' men and explained that after the funeral the Duke had begged Caldwell to acquire a fake will but he had been unable to do so. Mr Avory, in cross-examination, asked the elderly American whether he had heard of the 'Stewart Case' – a similar affair in New York. He had – indeed, he had been involved, offering to sell his story to the *New York Herald* for $10,000. It was at this point that the case was adjourned.

On the same day, in the perjury case a court found that a will left by Thomas was legal and Herbert was allowed to inherit the family's wealth. On 15th November Herbert made a rare appearance in court, by this time he was suffering from 'vein troubles' and was given an armchair from which to witness the scene. Caldwell was asked whether the Duke had been suffering from problems with his nose. "I treated the Duke for 60 days at the Bazaar," he replied. He went on to explain that the Duke had paid him £5,000 for the treatment and he described the building.
"And if this description is untrue, then your story must be untrue?" asked Horace Avory.
"Yes sir."
"You told us the Duke supervised the funeral."
"Yes sir."
"With whiskers on?"
"Yes sir."
"Black I suppose – for the funeral."
Laughter swept the courtroom.
"No sir – grey!," cackled the wily old man.

The 5th Duke of Portland

On November 19th Mary Robinson was called once more – this time, regarding the contents of her stolen diary. The hacks in the press gallery sharpened their pencils and this most colourful of witnesses didn't fail them. Robinson told the court that the diary included notes relating to her first meeting with the Duke. She had been walking in Hyde Park with Charles Dickens when they came across the Duke. Dickens introduced them and it was he who explained to her the truth of the Duke's double life! On November 28th Robinson was called once more but failed to show.

During December the number of court appearances began to fall although there were the first moves to exhume Druce's coffin but the cemetery owners, 'The London Cemetery Company' resisted the plan. They were concerned that if the coffin was full of lead weight and they had performed a full Christian burial for it they would be held up to mockery. Eventually though the order was granted and on December 30th the cemetery was closed to the public. Policemen guarded the gates. At 10.20am Professor Augustus Pepper of Saint Mary's Hospital, Paddington, stepped forward to examine the contents of the infamous casket.

Police guarding Highgate Cemetery

On December 31st the Druce's legal team met to discuss the findings. One and a half-hours later a public statement was issued to waiting reporters. It read, "The matter is still under consideration, no decision has been arrived at. The reports of the doctor and surveyor who attended the exhumation on Mr Druce's behalf have not yet been received. A further consultation has been booked for Saturday. The re-erection of the family monument and dismantling of the shed was completed yesterday afternoon."

On January 5th 1908 further talks were held for two hours. It was agreed that Atherley-Jones should alone decide the next move and the fate of the claim given that the coffin had indeed held a body. However, George's Australian solicitor immediately told the press that his client was satisfied that the body found in the casket was not that of Thomas Charles Druce. That afternoon, Herbert, now aged almost 62, appeared before Justice Plowden. He repeated that he had seen his father lying in the coffin, now over 40 years previously. Amongst the usual crowd of witnesses was one J.A.T. Good who, "appeared for a person interested" as the records of the time describe him.

Sir Charles Matthews called Leslie Robert Vigers, a member of the Institute of Surveyors who had witnessed the exhumation.

"How far down was the exhumation made?"
"There was no excavation. The marble kerbs were removed, but the vault was not opened."
"That was the point reached as the result of Sunday afternoon's work?"
"Yes."
"Did you attend again on Monday?"
"Yes."
"Was the site in the same condition?"
"It was."

Vigers had watched the stone slabs being rolled back, he saw Annie's coffin, which had been moved to one side. Beneath was a floor of eight York stone slabs about one and a half inches thick.
"The floor was removed to reveal an adult's and a child's coffin."
Although this reply wasn't questioned during the trial, it should have been. There was never a child's coffin in the vault. The only explanation other than foul play was that this was Walter's coffin. The adult coffin, explained Vigers, had a plate which read, 'Thomas Charles Druce, December 28th 1864, in his 71st year."
Mr Atherley-Jones now proceeded to cross-question the witness.
"Are you satisfied that both the grave and the coffin had not been tampered with?"
"Certainly."
"And that they pointed, so far as your judgement could go, to having been undisturbed since 1864?"
"Yes."
This was not so, with the burial of Walter in 1880 and Annie in 1893, the vault had been disturbed. Atherley-Jones picked up on this and Vigers admitted his mistake. Evidence on both sides seemed full of holes.

Next in the box was Professor Augustus Joseph Pepper of Saint Mary's Hospital and an adviser to the Home Office. He described the scene. Inside the wooden coffin was a sealed lead shell containing, "a human body covered by a shroud of white cambric, figured near the margin."
"Was there anything over the face?"
"A linen handkerchief with TCD and 12 embroidered on it."
Pepper described the body as, "a male body, aged."
"By 'aged', what do you mean?"
"I should say 65-75. Its height as it lay was five feet, seven and a half inches, allowing for three-quarters of an inch shrinkage after death, it

would make the man five feet, eight and a half inches. The body was good with the skin broken in one part."

"Was it good enough for the features to be recognised?"

"Oh, quite easily."

"Before you go on to describe the features, had you on you at the time, this photograph?"

"Yes, it is the photograph marked eight."

Mr Avory explained that the image was of Mr Druce, standing.

"With that photograph in your possession, did you form your view as to the identity of the body?"

"There was a striking resemblance....the head was covered with scanty reddish brown hair, a small part white. It was parted neatly over the left side. One side was brushed slightly over the forehead. The eyebrows were rather thick and wavy, with a reddish brown moustache, whiskers and beard with a good deal of white. The beard was bushy of coarse hair."

"The same as in the photograph?"

"Exactly. The lower trunk of the body was extremely decayed. The deceased having suffered from fistula and abscesses or some destructive diseases of that kind."

A photo of Druce

In fact, Druce had indeed suffered with abscesses for three months and gangrene for nine days prior to his demise.

"Did you look for chloride of lime?" asked Atherley-Jones.

"Yes, there were some traces about the middle of the body."

Plowden intervened. "I think I must ask you now, at this stage of the case what impression this evidence has made on your mind?"

Atherley-Jones insisted that Avory call all his witnesses before making a statement. So George William Thackrah of Finsbury Park was called. He had been a partner in Druce and Co., entering the business in May 1860.

Mr Thackrah began to go into Druce's business affairs when Atherley-Jones rose.

"I do not wish to burden my friend with this matter, I understood the evidence was to be in regard to the exhumation only."

Avory sharply retorted, "You must leave it to me to determine what is necessary."

Thackrah then revealed that he, one of Druce's oldest friends, had witnessed the exhumation and that he had no doubt the body in the casket was his dear partner.

Justice Plowden turned to the witness and looked him straight in the eye. "You recognised him beyond a shadow of doubt?"
"Oh yes, beyond a shadow of doubt. There is no doubt whatever about it."
The witness left the box and Atherley-Jones again rose. He turned to face the jury as his voice, almost a whisper, spoke those famous words; "Our case is withdrawn."
Plowden addressed Herbert Druce; "The court thanks you for having consented in the interest of justice to the desecration of your father's grave. You are now discharged."

George Hollamby Druce was outside the arm of the British legal system. Only Caldwell and Robinson were under threat of prosecution for perjury. Robert Caldwell fled to America where he was arrested pending deportation to London. On January 7th a Reuters telegram reached Britain, it read, "The federal authorities have been informed that Caldwell's condition is exceedingly grave and he is not expected to survive more than a few days. The question of his extradition is likely to be indefinitely adjourned." The compulsive con-man died a few days later.

On January 14th a compulsory winding-up order for the Druce-Portland Company was granted. Three days later, Detective Inspector Drew of Scotland Yard tracked down and arrested the elusive Mary Robinson on a charge of wilful and corrupt perjury. She appeared on January 27th before Sir A. de Rutzen at Bow Street charged with, "unlawfully, falsely, knowingly, wilfully and corruptly committing wilful and corrupt perjury". She pleaded not guilty however, the following day Reuters reported that two detectives were on their way to England with information about her past. At this news Robinson dismissed her legal team and changed her plea to guilty. On February 24th she was sent to jail.

George returned to Australia, Herbert died five years later in 1913 aged sixty-six, Louie pre-deceased him by three years and their children followed them into the Highgate vault in 1922 and 1932 respectively. Both dead before their fifty-fifth birthdays. Their tomb is now crowned by a circle of ivy and visited by many hundreds of tourists every year – a ghostly tribute to a family who brought a little mystery into people's lives. But it doesn't end there.

After the fuss had died down, a story began to circulate that Herbert had had his father's body moved from Kensal Green to Highgate prior to the exhumation. Remember that some of the evidence regarding possible tampering with the grave had been discredited in court. Witnesses came forward saying they had seen builders around the two plots. The claim was never taken seriously but who knows.....the mystery still, in part, lives on.

Above: Harcourt House, the home of the Cavendish family

Right: Much of the West End of London recalls the Duke of Portland's family

The cemetery with its own unique 'one-way' ticket!

Brookwood Cemetery in Surrey is Britain's largest burial place covering an astonishing 2000 acres. Founded in 1852 by the London Necropolis and National Mausoleum Company the neat manicured lawns, clumps of monkey puzzle trees and stunning architecture proved to be the perfect draw for the bereaved. This commercial operation was a major success and plots were sold to families from across the south of England - but how to transport the coffins and mourners down to rural Surrey, some 25 miles from London?

In November 1854 a unique railway line opened for business. Run by the cemetery's owners in conjunction with The London and South Western Railway this so-called 'Necropolis Railway' had its own station adjacent to Waterloo with a chapel, retiring rooms and even a bar which was rumoured to have had a sign bearing the legend 'spirits served here' over the door. Mourners would congregate here before being transported with the coffin on board a private train to the cemetery's own stations. A regular service continued until 1900 after which time the trains only ran when they were specially booked to do so and in 1902 the London station was completely rebuilt at 121 Westminster Bridge Road from where it continued to operate until it was hit by a bomb during the second world war.

The entrance to the London terminus survives today as does the track bed within the cemetery grounds. This must be one of the most unusual railway lines Britain has ever had - we wonder how many one-way tickets they sold.

THE LIFE OF JOHN DILLINGER
The folk-hero of the Great Depression

JOHN Herbert Dillinger was born in Oak Hill, Indianapolis, USA, on June 22nd, 1903, the second child of a prosperous grocer, also called John, and his wife Mary. His sister Audrey, who was fourteen years older, was soon to take the place of their mother when Dillinger was only three and Mary died.

Dillinger Senior, a God-fearing man, believed any show of affection towards his children was a weakness, thus he ruled them with a rod of iron. Despite this lack of affection publicly, Mr. Dillinger still cared about his son and daughter and did his best to bring them up with a Christian attitude to life and good manners. While he obviously failed with the former, he succeeded with the latter, for even young Dillinger's Sunday School teacher told the world that he would always raise his hat in her direction.

For all this show of manners it soon became evident to the residents of Oak Hill that Dillinger was heading for the wrong side of the law. When he was about ten years of age he became leader of a neighbourhood gang called 'The Dirty Dozen' which had started its existence as nothing special, but within a short time, due to Dillinger's intervention, soon became involved with petty crime. One of their sorties took them into property belonging to the Pennsylvania Railroad, where they stole tons of coal which they sold to Oak Hill residents.

At about the time Dillinger was getting into his first known criminal activity, his father re-married and within a few months his step-mother gave birth to a boy which was named Hubert. Dillinger immediately resented the attention shown to the baby and be began to spend more and more time with his closest friend Fred Brewer, himself the victim of a broken home.

To pass the time both boys would hang out in a veneer mill next door to Dillinger's father's grocery store, and it has been claimed that one afternoon after the mill closed for the day, John Dillinger and Fred Brewer tied another boy to a conveyor and then switched on a large circular saw, only switching it off when the terrified boy was within inches of death.

It has also been alleged that in 1916, when Dillinger was just a teenager, he and Brewer were responsible for organising a sexual attack on a local girl, and from this time Dillinger's sexual appetite became insatiable and he would spend plenty of time chasing any local girls who would tolerate his forward approach. When he failed with his attempted conquests in Oak Hill he would venture into Indianapolis itself where prostitutes were easier targets.

John Dillinger Senior, almost in despair at his son's tactics, sold his store and bought a farm in the country, hoping in vain that to be close to nature would have a rehabilitating effect on young Dillinger, but it was not to be.

In July 1923, Dillinger, now a tall, slim young man, had travelled into Indianapolis after stealing a car and the following morning he was found wandering in the streets by a policeman. Wary of vagrants the officer approached Dillinger:

"What are ya doin' here, boy?" he queried.
"Nothing much!" Dillinger replied.
"Where are you from?"
"Oak Hill," Dillinger said.
"Where've you been?" the cop queried.
"Oh, here and there, just looking around," came the reply.
The officer questioned Dillinger further and decided he wasn't happy with the answers he was getting, so he decided to escort the youth to the local police station to check out his story. He grabbed Dillinger by

the collar of his coat, but the wiry young thief slipped out of the coat and escaped. Aware that the law would soon be on his heels if he returned to his father's farm, Dillinger ran away and joined the US Navy, serving on USS Utah, but when that ship docked in Boston Dillinger went 'Absent Without Leave'

In April 1924 Dillinger returned to his father's farm with a pretty young girl he introduced as Beryl Hovius whom he then declared was his wife. His father was delighted and felt the responsibility of a wife would have a calming influence, but he was soon proved wrong. Within weeks Dillinger was in trouble with the law again, this time for stealing chickens, but he was lucky for his father used his influence and the case was dismissed.

Dillinger became friendly with a baseball umpire named Ed Singleton, and they soon set on a plan to make easy money. They learned that a prosperous grocer named B.F. Morgan always carried his takings with him on Saturday night when he went for a haircut. At approximately 8.30pm on Saturday, September 6th, 1924, Morgan, a big man, locked up his store and set off on his regular trip to his barber shop when he was approached by Dillinger who had left Singleton in a getaway car. Dillinger was carrying a .32 revolver in one hand and a blunt instrument in the other, with which he struck Morgan over the head, knocking him to the ground and robbing him of $500.

It wasn't long before the law caught up with the crook and Dillinger decided to plead guilty, believing he would receive a light sentence, especially if he named Singleton as his accomplice. But he was wrong, and instead he received a jail sentence of from ten to twenty years, while Singleton, who appeared before a different judge and pleaded not guilty, was sentenced to a term in prison of from two to fourteen years.

Dillinger (right) being arrested in 1934

Dillinger served nine years and was released on parole on May 22nd, 1933, just as the United States was in the middle of a wave of gangsterism, with prohibition and bank robberies commonplace. It did not take long for the young gangster Dillinger to get involved in the crime scene again, having learnt the ropes well during his spell in jail. He robbed a bank in Dalesville, Indiana, only eight weeks after his release, getting away with $3,500. Two weeks later he struck again with two companions at the First National Bank in Montpelier, this time getting more than $10,000. Within three months Dillinger and his gang had robbed banks to the tune of around $100,000 – or so it was claimed.

Within a year of his release from prison Dillinger had become a national figure, a folk hero to many Americans suffering in the wake of the Great Depression who saw him as a kind of latter-day Robin Hood. But his methods were not impressing law enforcement agencies throughout the country, especially J. Edgar Hoover's Federal Bureau of Investigation, for in his year of robbery the Dillinger gang had also shot and killed a Sheriff and a policeman.

J. Edgar Hoover

The net closed in on Dillinger on July 22nd, 1934, when he left the Biograph Cinema in Chicago after watching a gangster film, "Manhattan Melodrama", starring Clark Gable and William Powell. A total of sixteen FBI agents were waiting outside and as Dillinger reached the corner of an alleyway next to the National Food Store on North Lincoln Avenue, he appeared to sense something was wrong and his hand went into his coat to grab his gun. The FBI agents opened fire and four bullets struck the notorious gangster killing him instantly.

Dillinger was buried in Crown Hill Cemetery, Indianapolis, and because of the degree of curiosity a concrete slab was placed over his coffin to protect it from macabre souvenir hunters.

John Dillinger Senior later toured the USA giving lectures on the subject of 'Crime Doesn't Pay', unwittingly following in the footsteps of the legendary Frank James, brother of Jesse James, themselves notorious gangsters of a different era.

CHARLIE PEACE
A monster remembered

JUST before Charles Peace was executed he told a clergyman who was talking to him in prison that after he had died he hoped the notoriety of the name 'Charlie Peace' would die with him, and that the insatiable Victorian thrill seekers would forget he ever existed.

It was a wish he made in vain, for Peace will always be remembered by crime historians for the brilliance he displayed in his burglary antics, but also for the despicable lifestyle he led, particularly in the way he showed a totally callous streak in allowing others to take the blame for his misdeeds.

Peace was not born into a criminal family, as was so often the case in Victorian society, for his father, John Peace, started his working life as a collier, working in the pits of Burton-on-Trent, but after losing his leg in an accident he showed an amazing ability to adapt by joining Wombwell's Wild Beast Show as a lion tamer! Indeed if contemporary records are to be believed, John soon gained a reputation for being totally fearless in the face of such ferocious animals, particularly with his disability which must have had some effect on his agility.

But this work didn't last either, and John Peace gave up lion taming and went to work as a shoemaker in Sheffield, and it was here in Nursery Street, that Charles Peace entered the world on May 14th, 1832, the youngest of four children.

As he grew older, Charles was sent to school in Sheffield and soon found he had an aptitude for model making, taming cats, and the singularly unusual talent of throwing up a heavy ball of metal which he would then catch in a leather pouch fixed to his forehead!

At the age of fourteen he took a job in a rolling mill and had an accident which was to change his life. A piece of red-hot steel somehow entered his leg just below the knee and he spent the next eighteen months in Sheffield Infirmary. The injury, despite the length of time in hospital, left Peace a cripple for the rest of his life. To compound his problems at this time his father also died, leaving his teen years without male guidance and discipline, and this possibly changed his way of looking at life, which he must have regarded as dealing him a bad hand at such a young age.

We know nothing of what first started Peace on the road to crime, but his first exploit was stealing a gentleman's gold watch, before going on to greater and more notorious crimes. On October 26th, 1851, a house in Sheffield was broken into and property belonging to the lady of the house was stolen. Some of it was found in Peace's possession and he was arrested. No doubt due to having a good character at that time, and receiving a reference from his former employer at the rolling mill, Peace was let off with only one month in jail.

After his release Peace took up playing the violin, teaching himself to play an instrument with a single string, but his talent must have been considerable despite his lack of training and the deficit in the normal number of violin strings, for one contemporary report described him, perhaps somewhat romantically, as "the modern Paganini." But however good or bad he was at playing there is no doubt that the violin played an important part in his life, and he even played at fairs and in public houses.

During 1854 the homes of several wealthy residents in the Sheffield area were burgled and plenty of valuable items taken which were later traced to Peace and he was arrested again. With him this time was his married sister, Mary Ann Neil, and a woman he had been courting for some time. On October 20th, 1854, Peace was sentenced in Doncaster to four years penal servitude, while his female companions, who had been found in possession of the stolen goods, were sentenced to six months each.

After serving his sentence, Peace resumed violin playing, but it was now a cover up to his full-time occupation of burglary, and his nefarious operations extended well beyond the boundaries of his home town, and on the night of August 11th, 1859, a house in Manchester was broken into and quite a booty of valuable goods taken which, for some reason, was discovered the following day concealed in a hole in the middle of a field. The police left the items where they were and waited and when the burglar finally collected his haul and police sprung out of hiding, it was Peace who was taken into custody after a violent struggle. For this episode he was sentenced to six years penal servitude, despite an attempt by his aged mother to try to provide a perjurous alibi for him.

It was 1864 before Charles Peace was back in circulation again and he returned to Sheffield, though it wasn't long before he crossed the Pennines once more to Manchester and up to his old tricks again. In 1866 he was captured in the act of burglary in a house in Lower Broughton and this time for his sins, on December 3th, 1866, at Manchester Assizes, he was sentenced to eight years.

After his release Peace travelled back to Sheffield where he joined his family. By this time he was married with a son, having wed a widow named Hannah Ward in 1859, but frequently leaving her as he visited Britain's prisons. Shortly after his wedding Hannah had given birth to a daughter, and during his fourth imprisonment she had a son, but he died before Peace was released from prison and he never saw the child.

For the next three years little criminal activity was attributed to Peace who found work as a picture framer, a task he found he was particularly good at, and his wife and family must have thought they were now in for a stable period of domesticity, but when Peace moved them all from Sheffield city centre to the district of Darnell in 1875, circumstances were to take a turn for the worse, a turn which was ultimately to have tragic consequences.

It was in Darnell that Peace met Arthur and Katherine Dyson, who lived a few doors away in Britannia Road, and soon short, ugly Charlie Peace and six foot tall, distinguished looking Arthur Dyson and his wife were friends. Katherine Dyson was described as a "buxom and blooming" woman, about twenty-five-years old and attractive, and it seems from statements later made by Peace, though denied by Katherine, that they became lovers. But despite Mrs Dyson's assertions that this was untrue, circumstantial evidence in the form of photographs taken of them together, the fact that Peace gave her a ring, and that he took her to music halls and public houses without her husband, points to the idea that Peace was telling the truth.

It was a fateful relationship, for soon it became apparent that Peace was either infatuated with Katherine or wished to dominate her totally, as he allegedly did with his wife, to whom he introduced his 'mistress'. But the infatuation, or whatever it was, did not run deep through Mrs Dyson's veins for she was soon complaining that Peace was a demon, "beyond the power of even a Shakespeare to paint" who pestered her constantly with his demands, and it did not take long before Peace was being accused of making the life of Mr and Mrs Dyson unbearable. Though to Peace himself, he was the victim and he described himself as a "slighted lover who had been treated with contumely and ingratitude."

It appears that six foot tall Mr. Dyson was scared of Peace, despite his diminutive size, for the next attempt to keep him away from his wife and himself was a strange one of throwing a note into Peace's garden upon which was written: "Charles Peace is requested not to interfere with my family." A couple of days later the pair met in the street and Peace tried to trip up his neighbour, and the same night he came across Mrs Dyson who was talking to friends, and Peace threatened to blow out her brains and those of her husband. Mr. Dyson took out a summons against Peace, but before he could be arrested the aggressive little crook left Darnell and travelled to Kingston-upon-Hull, where he opened an eating house which was run by his wife.

From Hull, Peace made his way to Manchester, which seemed to hold a peculiar attraction to him, and it was here that he committed his first murder. He entered the grounds of a house belonging to Samuel Greatorex on the boundary of Whalley Range and Chorlton, about four miles south of the city centre, at about midnight on August 1st, 1876. Unfortunately for Peace he was seen by two constables, and one of them, PC Nicholas Cock, cornered him.

"Stand still, I want a word with you," Cock said.
Peace replied by pulling out a revolver. "Out of my way, or I'll shoot!"

Cock, with the bravado verging on madness which characterized British policemen of the time, drew his truncheon and confronted Peace as though the gun did not exist.
"Put down the gun and don't be foolish," he said, and made for his foe.

Desperate to escape, Peace fired twice, the first shot going wide of the constable, but seeing that he was still coming forward the second shot hit him and fatally wounded him. Not waiting for Cock's colleague to come on the scene, Peace made off into the night and returned to Hull, where, to his astonishment but delight, he heard that two brothers, William and John Habron, had been arrested and charged with Cock's murder.

The shooting of PC Cock

The brothers lived close to the scene of the killing, and on November 27th their trial started before Mr. Justice Lindley at Manchester Assizes. At once John Habron was acquitted, but the case against his brother depended on the fact that he had been heard making threats against Cock. The late PC was only twenty-three years of age and earlier in the summer he had taken out summonses against both brothers for being drunk and disorderly, and William Habron had threatened to "do for the little bobby."

On July 27th, William had been fined five shillings (25p), a considerable sum for a working man, while four days later on August 1st, John Habron was fined half a sovereign (50p), which was more than half a week's wages for the average man, and as nurserymen working in Whalley Range at the time, it is certain that both brothers fitted into this category.

Between the two dates the Habron brothers had been overheard making threats, but other information relied on by the prosecution was that William Habron had made inquiries at a gunsmiths about the price of cartridges a couple of days before Cock's murder, and two cartridge percussion caps had been found in the pocket of a waistcoat belonging to William Habron which he had been given by his employer. His employer compounded the problem by giving evidence that the percussion caps could not have been there when he gave away the waistcoat.

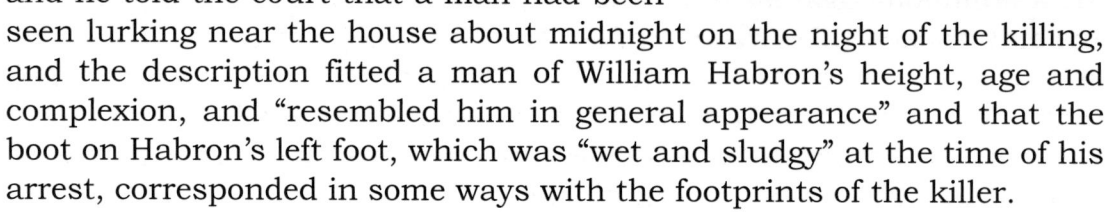

The constable with Cock also gave evidence and he told the court that a man had been seen lurking near the house about midnight on the night of the killing, and the description fitted a man of William Habron's height, age and complexion, and "resembled him in general appearance" and that the boot on Habron's left foot, which was "wet and sludgy" at the time of his arrest, corresponded in some ways with the footprints of the killer.

Contemporary sketch of PC Nicholas Cock

It was altogether a rather shabby trial, and even the judge was not impressed with the case for the prosecution, and pointed out that the evidence was weak and had not been proven. With regard to the footprint, what was there to prove that it had been made on the night of the murder? If it had been made the previous day, then the defence had proved that it could not have been the suspect's. In addition, it was pointed out, Habron had a previous good character, notwithstanding the drunk and disorderly charge, that he had been in bed when arrested and no firearms had been traced to him. Despite the summing up, however, William was found guilty of Cock's murder but the jury recommended mercy. Mr Justice remained silent until he donned the infamous black triangle of cloth and handed down the sentence of "death by hanging."

On December 6th, a meeting attended by forty influential Manchester residents, described as "gentlemen from the town," met to petition the Home Secretary to reconsider the sentence, and two days before the execution Habron was given a reprieve with his sentence being changed to one of penal servitude for life.

All of this was music to the ears of Charles Peace who loved attending trials, and it shows the callous disregard that he had for his fellow men because he sat in the Manchester court for the trial and must have smirked to himself when he heard Habron sentenced to death for a murder he himself had committed. If the execution had gone ahead there is no doubt that Peace would have remained tight-lipped and would have seen an innocent man executed, which would have made him guilty of double murder!

After the trial Peace returned to Sheffield and started pestering Mrs Dyson and her husband again, much to their chagrin, for they thought he had left the city and gone away for good, and they had even moved to the district of Banner Cross to evade him. But no such luck was to befall them, for Peace was still wrathful of the way Mr. Dyson had taken out a summons against him, and he meant to take his revenge and to this end tracked them down. Indeed the lure of the Dyson's was so irresistible that it suggests paranoia on the part of Peace, who watched their home and waited until Mrs Dyson came out of the back door. She went into an outhouse but on emerging she found herself facing Peace who was holding his revolver in his hand.

Mrs Dyson, in her terror, screamed and ran back into the outhouse. Her husband hearing the noise, came quickly out of the house and Peace later said: "As soon as I saw him I immediately started down the passage which leads to the road. Before I could do so, Mr. Dyson seized me. I struggled to get past him. I said: 'Stand back and let me go,' but he did not do so, and I fired one barrel of my revolver wide at him, to frighten him...I could have shot him dead at the first shot had I cared to do so, I was so near to him. He had got hold of the arm to which I had strapped my revolver, and then I knew I had not a moment to spare.

"I made a desperate effort, wrenched the arm from him, and fired again. It was a life and death struggle, but even then I did not intend to shoot Mr. Dyson. My blood was up, and, having fired one shot, I knew if I was captured it would mean transportation for life. That made me determined to get off. I fired again, but with no intention of killing him. I saw Mr. Dyson fall. I did not know where he was hit or that his wound was one that would prove fatal. All that was in my head was to get away, and if we had not struggled I should have got away without this."

Mrs Dyson hearing the shots and fearing the worst rushed out of the outhouse to her husband's side and shouted: "Murder! You villain, you have shot my husband!" Two hours later Arthur Dyson died from his injuries.

A hue and cry was soon raised for the arrest of Charles Peace and a £100 reward was put on his head and police circulated the following impressive description:

"Charles Peace, wanted for murder on the night of the 29th inst. He is thin and slightly built, from fifty-five to sixty years of age. Five feet four inches or five feet high; grey (nearly white) hair, beard and whiskers. He lacks use of three fingers on left hand, walks with his legs rather wide apart, speaks somewhat peculiarly as though his tongue were too large for his mouth, and is a great boaster. He is a picture-frame maker. He occasionally cleans and repairs clocks and watches and sometimes deals in oleographs, engravings and pictures. He has been in penal servitude for burglary in Manchester. He has lived in Manchester, Salford, and Liverpool and Hull."

The description, thorough as it seems, had to be altered later for it was discovered that Peace, despite looking older, was only forty-four years old at the time and not the "fifty-five to sixty" outlined in the notice.

Peace was perpetually on the move after the killing and he travelled from Hull to Doncaster, then to London and Bristol and at the beginning of January 1877 left Bristol for Bath. He also travelled from Bath to Oxford in the company of a police sergeant, who had a female prisoner in his charge, and the extent of Peace's brass-necked attitude was confirmed when they discussed the case on the journey and Peace later commented: "He seemed a smart chap, but not smart enough to know me!"

From Oxford he went to Birmingham, where he stayed a few days, before moving on to Derby, where he also stayed a few days and finally arrived in Nottingham. Here he found lodgings with a Mrs Adamson, a receiver of stolen goods, in The Marsh, a low class area of the town, and it was here that he met thirty-five-years old Susan Bailey, who was to become his mistress and later was to betray him to searching police officers.

Susan Bailey, if indeed that was her real name, had been in, what was described as, a "chequered marriage" and she continued to receive a weekly allowance from her husband even after their parting, but on taking up with Peace she somewhat mysteriously changed her name again and became known to all and sundry as simply "Mrs Thompson."

Life in Nottingham continued with a series of burglaries carried out by Peace, and in June, 1877, he was almost caught stealing blankets, but by waving his trusty and deadly revolver about, he was able to escape and soon afterwards Peace and Thompson made their way to Hull where they took rooms, in typical Peace brazenness, in the house of a police sergeant to whom he said he was an agent!

It soon became clear to the sober citizens of Hull that there was a burglar with singular talent in their town, for many homes belonging to local councillors and wealthy merchants were soon on his tally, and it became obvious even to Peace that a cooling down period was needed so he took his mistress back to Nottingham where he soon found a £50 reward was placed on his capture. But lady luck was still with him at this stage, and he had an amazing piece of this luck on one occasion when detectives came into the couple's bedroom and found them in bed together.

The detectives asked Peace his name and he told them he was John Ward, a hawker of spectacles, and he refused to get out of bed and dress until the officers were out of the room. They obliged and went downstairs to await his convenience, and Peace seized his chance and left the house and disappeared to another part of Nottingham. He later sent Mrs Thompson a note telling her to join him, and the two of them made off again, calling briefly in Hull but after seeing his wife's eating place was still being watched by detectives, he decided the best place for Mrs Thompson and himself was the smoky realms of London, with its four million inhabitants.

Over the next two years Peace tackled the London scene with gusto, and in that comparatively short period of time his nefarious activities netted him enough money to move from poor, obscure lodgings to more elegant surroundings at 25 Stangate Street, Lambeth, where he set himself up as a dealer in musical instruments but which, in reality, was a front for his criminal activities.

Indeed so successful did his criminal activities within the capital become that by Christmas 1877 he invited his now grown up daughter and her fiancé, a man named Bolsover, to join him and Mrs Thompson, and he was soon showing them the sights of the heart of the British Empire, wearing top hat and top quality clothing, but still showing a foolhardy spirit by asking passing policemen for directions from time to time, as though testing their powers of observation.

As he prospered Peace decided it would be a good idea to have Mrs Thompson and his wife Hannah and their son live under the same roof, so a much more resplendent property was found in Crane Court, Greenwich, and before long he also took adjoining properties in Billingsgate Street in the same area, which he furnished with some style, but even this arrangement did not last long before they all moved to 5 East Terrace, Evelina Road, Peckham, for which Peace paid £30 a year rent.

So confident had Peace become by this time that the good life would continue that he even obtained permission to build a stable adjoining the property for his pony and trap, and to make sure there was no problem with references he invited the estate agent to dinner at his Greenwich home, and the latter was evidently so impressed that the subject of references was soon forgotten.

The Peckham house was described as a suburban villa, with a basement, ground floor, upper floor, and a bow window to the front sitting room, with a garden at the back which ran down to the Chatham and Dover railway line. Altogether a most desirable residence for a 'businessman' who just happened to be a master criminal.

The domestic arrangements were extraordinary to be sure, for his legal wife, Hannah, and son Willie, lived in the basement and became known in the neighbourhood as Mrs and Master Ward, while Peace and his mistress, occupied the best rooms on the ground floor and were known as "Mr and Mrs Thompson" to their neighbours.

Life seemed pleasant at last for Peace and he even devoted some of his attention to inventions, and in association with a man called Henry Brion he patented an invention for raising sunken vessels, and the *Patent Gazette* records:

'2635 Henry Fersey Brion, 22 Philip Road, Peckham Rye, London, S.E., and John Thompson, 5 East Terrace, Evelina Road, Peckham Rye, London, S.E., for an invention for raising sunken vessels by the displacement of water within the vessels by air and gas'

Peace also used his considerable imagination and intelligence to invent a smoke helmet for firemen, and an improved brush for washing railway carriages, and it is all the more astonishing that this little man was guilty of murdering two innocent men.

But, like all good things that come to an end, the peaceful co-existence within Peace's home was soon to draw to a close and lead to his downfall. Mrs Thompson was often the worst for drink and she was regularly in the unfortunate position of slipping out of the house in her drunken state and chatting to neighbours, a certain prescription for danger if ever there was one since she knew so much about Peace's secret life. Peace often lost his temper with his mistress cum 'wife' and gave her beatings if she stepped out of line, but at the same time he had a soft spot for her and could never deny her anything; indeed he was once quoted as saying: "she could swim in gold if she liked!"

Between the beginning of 1877 and October 1878 Peace operated in London with a degree of success unlike any other burglar, but tension at home between his two mistresses could have caused him to make what became a fatal mistake and at two o'clock on the morning of October 10th, 1878, a police constable named Robinson saw a light appear at the back of a house in St John's Park, Blackheath, and he called two colleagues to the scene, one of whom waited in the road, the second going to the front of the house, while Robinson went into the back garden. Hardly had he arrived on the scene before the constable saw a figure climbing out of the dining room window and moving down the path.

As Robinson moved forward Peace saw him and turned and, true to form, pulled out his revolver. "Keep back, or, by God, I'll shoot you!" he said. What followed next was a familiar situation, for PC Robinson kept coming and Peace fired no less than five shots, three passing close to the policeman's head, one missing by a wider margin, but the fifth hitting him in the arm, close to his elbow. In spite of the wound, however, Robinson tackled the burglar and flung him to the ground, grabbing the deadly revolver until his colleagues rushed up and grabbed hold of Peace.

Next morning Peace appeared in Greenwich Police Court, but even then his identity was unknown, and he was remanded in custody for a week and he was eventually charged under the name of John Ward and was sentenced to penal servitude for life for attempted murder.

His true identity may never have been known had not police spoken to Mrs Thompson, for it did not take long for her true character to show through and she, possibly inspired by the £100 reward, decided to give them chapter and verse what information they needed, namely, of course, that their 'John Ward' was none other than the most wanted man in Britain at that time – Charlie Peace.

Police were jubilant. Scotland Yard had captured the country's most infamous killer, and even the parochial Sheffield Constabulary joined in the celebrations at the news that their unsolved murder of Arthur Dyson was about to become one step nearer being marked 'solved', and in anticipation of the day a detective was sent by the quickest ship that could be found to America to see Katherine Dyson, who had moved there following her husband's murder two years previously, as she would be the main witness for the prosecution.

The trial got under way at Leeds Assizes at last and after the normal process of law it ended several days later on the afternoon of February 4th, 1879. After hearing the evidence of Mrs Dyson and Robinson, the arresting officer who had by then been promoted to sergeant, the jury took just twelve minutes to return their verdict – "Guilty."

The judge, Mr. Justice Lopes, addressed Peace and said: "It is not my duty, still less is it my desire to aggravate your feelings at this moment by recapitulating any part of the details of what I fear I can only call your criminal career." He then donned the feared black cap and sentenced Peace to death by hanging and added by way of comment: " I implore you during the short time which may remain to you in life to prepare for eternity."

During his stay in prison awaiting his execution, he admitted his part in the murder of PC Cock in Manchester, telling the Rev. J.H. Littlewood, vicar of Darnell, the Sheffield suburb to which Peace had indicated he wanted to be buried: "I want to tell you, to unburden my mind to you. I am about to die and I want to take from my conscience some things which weigh heavily upon it, and I am anxious to speak the truth, and nothing but the truth." He then told the vicar about his involvement with the Manchester burglary and subsequent killing of the constable and added somewhat bizarrely: " I want to tell you that I always made it a rule during the whole course of my career never to take life if I could avoid it.

"Whether you believe it or not, I never wanted to murder anybody. I only wanted to do what I came to do and get away, and it does seem odd after all that in the end I should have to be hanged for taking life, the very thing I was always so anxious to avoid." After Peace's confession the innocent William Habron was freed from jail, given a free pardon and compensation of £800.

On the morning of his execution, Tuesday, February 25th, 1879, Peace awoke at just before six o'clock and an hour or so later he ate a hearty breakfast of eggs, bacon and toast, washed down with plenty of tea, and shortly before eight o'clock walked steadily to the scaffold, and tried to refuse the traditional blindfold of the condemned man with the words: "Don't, I want to look." But the executioner William Marwood, a Lincolnshire shoemaker by trade, the

The hanging of Charlie Peace

man who invented the so-called 'long drop' which was more scientific in its despatch of those being hanged, carried out his duty to the letter and on the stroke of eight o'clock he pulled the lever which sent Peace to eternity. His body was buried within Armley Jail, and Charles Peace, at only forty-seven years of age, went down into the annals of criminal infamy.

The cover of just one publication that glamourised the life of Charlie Peace

Rat catching 'on the quiet!'

Elsewhere in this book we refer to many of the activities Victorian public houses were famous for - and it wasn't just boozing. Henry Mayhew, that most famous chronicler of Britain's underbelly, recorded details of the joys of rat-killings. He reports a conversation with one Jimmy Shaw, a London inn-keeper famous for staging rat baiting events as public entertainment.

Shaw purchased his rats from farmers and country folk who would go about collecting them once the harvest was safely gathered in. Seemingly, at one time farmers had paid yokels to catch rats, paying them twopence for each one caught on their land. The dead rats were then nailed up on a wall for all to see. When rat-killings became a popular pastime all this changed and the villagers would catch the rats for free taking them into towns and cities where landlords paid threepence a go.

Large establishments, Mayhew notes, would buy something in the region of 26,000 live rats a year charging customers to bring their dogs along to kill the creatures. Jimmy Shaw is quoted as saying: "Some first-class chaps will come here in the daytime and they'll try their dogs. They'll say, "Jimmy, give the dog 100." After he's polished them off they'll say, perhaps "Hang it, give him another 100." Shaw also let slip that some of his customers were noble and titled ladies who came to watch the sport - "on the quiet, you know!"

The World of Crime

HENRI LANDRU
The despicable crimes of the French Bluebeard

HENRI Landru was hardly what could be called a handsome man. His long, unkempt beard and moustache, prominent nose and bald head would have suggested, to those who observed him, a pleasant, middle-aged man, far removed from the deadly Romeo he actually was. A Romeo who, before being caught, would kill 10 women and a young boy!

Landru, a garage owner, was born in Paris on April 12th, 1869, and although his early years are obscure, his middle years became more than prominent to at least 283 women he allegedly seduced, or, as the jury at his trial heard, "had relations" with, which meant the same thing to a man of Landru's passionate nature.

Nicknamed 'Bluebeard', Landru was actually to become known to most of his victims and their near relatives under a complex miscellany of pseudonyms, including Dupont, Fremyet, Cruchet, and the ironically named Diard.

His first murder, so far as we know, took place in January 1915, when he killed his 'fiancée', a woman named Cruchet. He also killed her young son. It was the start of a killing career that was to be as cool and clear headed as it is possible to be. In other words, Landru killed without compassion, his immediate advantage being the cash he siphoned out of his victims. Indeed, from all accounts, Landru's main purpose in life was extortion, with sexual conquest a necessary but pleasant bonus to his plan.

He placed advertisements in Paris newspapers, including the morning paper *Le Journal*, in which he claimed he was a widower, aged 43, with two children. He also claimed to have a comfortable income and desired to meet a widow with a view to marrying her. According to some accounts he received almost 300 replies, all of which he carefully noted and ultimately categorised by potential wealth. His cold, carefully calculated plan was starting to work.

Such was the nature of Henri Landru's character that we have no real insight into the mind of this killer. Not for him the obviously blatant and psychopathic bragging; the letters to police; the teasing of his eventual captors. He kept calm and escaped capture for four years, and even then he gave very little away to the listening court.

More killings followed in the same year, including those of Madame Laborde-Line in June, and Madame Guillin in August. Both women were singularly unattractive and would have provided perfect prey for a fraudster such as Bluebeard, with his charming manner and glib tongue. Landru killed his first victims in a villa at Vernouille, and shortly afterwards moved to another villa in the village of Gambais, south of Paris. It was here that he killed a further seven women.

Paris, the city of lovers, was always the rendezvous for Landru and his new, lonely, mistresses. He would wine them and dine them, propose marriage, and take the women back to his villa in Gambais, paying for a return ticket for himself and a single ticket for his victim.

Despite Landru installing a stove in the villa, into which he shoved his murdered victims, thus producing vast quantities of smoke, neighbours were tolerant enough not to let this inconvenience them enough to be suspicious. So, for four years, Landru was able to lead his amazingly complex life.

But with the best of plans, a tiny mistake can lead to disaster, and this is exactly what happened to Landru. In his desire to gather wealth from his unsavoury trade he overlooked one vital factor. If people go missing there is usually someone left wondering what happened to the missing person. One such person left wondering was a woman called Madame Pelat, whose sister Anna Colomb, a forty-four-year old widow, had suddenly disappeared after answering an advertisement in a Paris newspaper. The same advertisement placed by Landru, then operating under the name Monsieur Fremyet. He met Anna Colomb, took her to his villa, then did not object when she invited Madame Pelat to visit her. By this simple oversight, Landru had, for the first time, allowed an outsider to come face to face with him, and subsequently identify him.

The villa at Gambais used by Landru

During this meeting Landru, or Monsieur Fremyet, had calmed the initial fears of Madame Pelat by saying he intended to marry Anna, but shortly afterwards the pair disappeared. Madame Pelat, having later sent a letter to her sister and having received no reply, contacted the mayor of the village asking if he knew of Anna's whereabouts. By coincidence, the mayor had also received a similar letter from the sister of another missing woman, Celestine Buisson, which stated that she had visited the villa in Gambais and had not been heard from since.

A meeting followed between the two concerned women and they compared notes. It did not take long to establish that Anna and Celestine had been courted and promised marriage by the same man. The authorities were now alerted and since they were also greatly concerned about a number of other missing women, they made a simple deduction that gave them reason for suspecting Landru, albeit that they did not know his real name at the time.

A further coincidence, however, was ultimately responsible for Landru being arrested. Celestine's sister, Mlle Lacoste, happened to be walking down a Paris street when she spotted the unmistakable figure of Landru, known to her as Monsieur Duport, entering a shop with another young woman. Mlle Lacoste went at once to the police with the information, and shortly afterwards Landru was traced to an apartment at 76 Rue de Rochechouart where he was living under the assumed name of Lucien Guillet. On his arrest, Landru protested his innocence to the murder charge which followed, and he claimed he was a simple engineer.

French police made a search of the apartment and found what was damning evidence. This was a notebook in which was listed Landru's carefully kept record of expenses incurred during his romantic interludes. Listed among those expenses was the evidence that he had only bought one way tickets to Gambais for Celestine Buisson and Anna Colomb. Other statistics soon came to light, including Landru's meticulously kept record of replies to his newspaper advertisements, with each woman carefully categorised according to wealth and expectations.

Landru in the dock

As the investigation continued, police were soon able to link Landru with his various aliases and his various retreats, including the villas at Gambais and Vernouille. It did not take long to find the stove that had emitted so much smoke into the French countryside, and the police were quick to find a large collection of human bones as well as items of jewellery and buttons. The four year killing spree of Henri Landru was over.

At his trial Landru kept his composure and claimed he was innocent of murder. It was a fruitless claim and after 90 minutes of debate the jury returned to the courtroom and found him guilty, but with a recommendation of mercy. The court President was unimpressed with the recommendation and sentenced Landru to death by guillotine, the execution to be carried out in public in front of the prison.

On the morning of February 23rd, 1922, Henri Landru, wearing a pair of dark trousers and a white, open necked shirt, was led shivering to the point of execution. The shivering was caused through a cold wind and not, apparently, through fear on the part of the condemned man. To the end he kept his composure, having refused the traditional cigarette, glass of rum and the services of a priest. Within seconds Henri Landru, the French Bluebeard, was dead.

What went on after closing time?

Being a department store owner in Victorian Britain gave one a certain status - department stores were often very grand affairs with sweeping staircases and of course, all the very latest fashions and mod cons. In London's Bayswater district the premier store was Whiteley's of Westbourne Grove which opened its doors in 1863. William Whiteley, its founder, was born in Wakefield, West Yorkshire in 1831. He began his career as a draper's assistant eventually buying his own property and gradually adding and adding to his empire. By 1876 he had his own thriving store with 17 departments employing several hundred staff.

But in his private life all was not well! During the 80s his properties were the subject of repeated arson attacks and there were rumours of several mistresses tucked up in flats across the capital. Whiteley though lived quietly on a secluded farm seeming to keep himself very much to himself and shunning the spotlight. But it was not to be. On a grey, wet afternoon in January 1907 Horace Rayner burst into Whiteley's office, over the ornate store, and began waving a gun about. The 76-year-old tycoon begged for mercy but Rayner shot him twice and he fell fatally wounded to the floor. The assassin told police that he was Whiteley's illegitimate son but we shall never be certain just what had been going on after closing time.

Broadway, New York, as it looked at the turn of the 20th century

The World of Crime

CAESAR AND THE SHOWGIRL
The murder of Caesar Young

NEW York at the turn of the 20th century - a heady mix of filthy lucre, corrupting power and success. America was a truly dynamic country but prosperity could act as a poison as well as an encouragement and so it was for many a showgirl who came into contact with a wealthy besotted patron. Take Evelyn Nesbit, whose story is recounted later in these pages, and who found herself embroiled in one of America's biggest sexual scandals.

Poor Evelyn began her career in the chorus of the touring musical "Floradora" alongside one Nan Patterson. Just like Evelyn, Nan was to meet and fall in love with a successful society figure. Nan was just twenty-two in 1904 when she fell for man about town Francis Young, known to his many horse-racing friends as 'Caesar'. Young's attentions and the many expensive gifts he lavished on her flattered Nan, a girl from a humble country background. Whilst Nan was impressed, Mrs Young was certainly not!

Eventually, tiring of the gossip surrounding her husband and marriage, Mrs Young decided that the only way she could split Caesar from his mistress was to take him out of the country. It was with this plan in mind that she booked a trip to Europe by liner, a trip that was intended to cool Nan's ardour. Unfortunately, things didn't quite go to plan.

When Mrs Young broke the holiday idea to her errant husband he took it all in his stride and agreed to go but not until he could see his mistress and explain his decision. What he intended to tell Nan, we shall never know. The lovers took a romantic cab ride through the theatre district of Broadway, while Mrs Young sat at home no doubt wondering whether her husband would return to her. After half an hour or so a shot rang out from the interior of the coach, a passer-by heard Nan shout, "Look at me Frank. Why did you do it?". The startled coachman was ordered by the chorus girl to go to the nearest drugstore, then she changed her mind ordering him to the hospital but it was too late - when they arrived, Francis Young's body fell out of the open door. There was a fatal bullet-wound to his chest, his shirt was soaked with blood and the murder weapon, a gun, was found in his pocket.

In November 1904 Nan Patterson stood trial for murder, the case hinging on the idea that she had shot her lover for deciding to leave her. The case however, was to be abandoned when one of the jury died and the trial was put on hold for a month. At the second trial, a couple of months later, the jury were unable to reach a verdict so again, Nan was to be kept waiting. In 1905 the court resumed again amid great public interest in whether Nan would go to the electric chair. Once again, the jury was unable to agree on an outcome so ten days later, the judge freed the suspect and Nan escaped with her life.

Across America children learnt a new playground chant -
Nan is free, Nan is free,
She escaped the electric chair,
Now she's out in the open air!

THAT'S YOUR FUNERAL
The Victorian and Edwardian Undertaker

THE middle of the nineteenth century proved a defining moment in the history of funeral directing. An emotional report by Edwin Chadwick into the state of public health which was published in 1843 had highlighted many of the appalling conditions experienced at city centre burial grounds and for the first time, private companies began opening cemeteries, often on a grand scale.

These new cemeteries were formed on the outskirts of major conurbations largely with one eye on public health concerns but the other firmly focused on profit. In order to attract the wealthiest customers they allowed the architects free-reign to design and lay out such delights as Egyptian-themed avenues, colonnades, catacombs and other fashionable extravaganzas. It is indeed true that the great Victorian cemeteries acted on three levels - repositories for the deceased, public parks and places of curiosity.

In the funeral trade changes were also being made and businesses found themselves also falling into one of three categories - coffin makers, undertakers who made coffins and carried out the arrangements and funeral furnishers who bought in the coffin and then offered an organising service. By the 1860's funerals were costing anything between £5. 19s. 0d and £15. 16s. 0d often giving a funeral director a mark-up of 175 - 500%! It is also true to say that undertakers were, on the whole, a rather old-fashioned and often greedy bunch with little co-operation between them and no interest in the development of their profession or services. Indeed, it was to be as late as 1898 before moves were made to establish any kind of trade association.

During our period of interest, funerals tended to be grand affairs with copious coffin-bearers, plumes of black feathers, men in elaborate scarves and so on, all with a heritage firmly rooted in heraldic history. Coffins were made of wood and lead and often covered in coloured felts and velvets - midnight blue, scarlet, black and holly green being particularly popular for adults with white or turquoise for children. Infants of course also had their own particular funereal traits - child mutes as depicted so memorably in Dicken's *Oliver Twist*, white gloved funeral directors and lockets of hair worn by grieving mothers. At the opposite end of the scale paupers, public or parish funerals were devoid of any frippery and coffins were loaded one on top of the other in mass graves. Organising this cheap form of funeral for a loved one caught out many a murderer with shallow pockets!

Other changes during this time were the ceasing of the undertaker walking in front of the hearse from the home to the cemetery in the 1880's, glass sided funeral cars were introduced from the 1870's, motorised hearses from 1900 (although the first silent one able to travel at a walking pace was not introduced until 1910) and train conveyed funerals from 1850. Yes, indeed, funeral parties often travelled from London to the London Necropolis and National Mausoleum Company's cemetery in Surrey by train - in fact, the company owned its own branch line, waiting rooms and chapel near Westminster and remained popular for almost forty years until it closed in 1941. It is still tradition that train transports the bodies of deceased monarchs.

Until the 1880's there was a great deal of anxiety about being buried alive. It certainly wasn't uncommon for people to request that they lie in state for several weeks before burial - just in case and this is partly what undertakers used their chapels of rest for. It is also said that there were frequent requests for the severing of an artery to ensure the corpse was properly deceased. In the early 1880's arterial embalming was introduced which gave a comfort of sorts - if you weren't already dead, you certainly soon would be.

The World of Crime

HE COULDN'T REMEMBER HIS VICTIM
The hanging of John Owen

AS in many of these cases, we start with a man about whom we know very little, other than that he used several names and that he was in trouble with the law from an early age. In this case, John Owen, or John Jones as he sometimes called himself, was released from Reading Gaol on the morning of 20th May 1870, having served one of a number of custodial sentences . He was to be dead within three months.

Within hours he was across the Berkshire border and into Middlesex, having made for the market town of Uxbridge, now a dot on the end of the London Underground map. He found lodgings in a wreck of a place, what was known politely as 'tramps lodgings' - a place to get sleep and little else. His first night of freedom was spent in filthy conditions, surrounded by a motley collection of misfits. There was little time for rest as John ran through his plans - for revenge.

The following night he set out to Denham, approximately a mile and a half away, arriving there at around 5am on the morning of Sunday 22nd May. He stole through the dark to the cottage of Edward Marshall where he bludgeoned him to death with a sledgehammer. Marshall's body was abandoned in the smithy before Owen slaughtered six other members of the family with an axe as they tried to make their escape.

Owen was soon apprehended by the police who established that the Marshall family had previously employed him. Whilst repairing a cart he had burst the tyres and thus was sacked, a fight had ensued and Owen had struck Mr Marshall about the eye before running off. Now, some three years later, he had come back to take his revenge. The police were also able to fill in some of the detail of Owen's past life - at one time he had run a beershop in Shipston-on-Stour but had lost his licence through keeping a disorderly house. He had also abandoned his wife before turning to a life of crime.

Owen enraged Victorian society who thought that his murderous spree was symptomatic of the way law and order was breaking down. The case became a hot topic of conversation and he was tagged 'The Denham Murderer'. Whilst in custody it was normal to be visited by a priest, but at first Owen refused all religious counsel. Eventually he declared himself to be a Roman Catholic and a clergyman was sent for to whom Owen made a confession - that he was only sorry he hadn't killed a policeman and a judge who had caught him for an earlier crime.

Owen's indifference didn't exactly endear him to the public and when his wife and father reported that as they sat crying in his cell he had said, "What have you to snivel for?", there were open calls for a swift hanging. After the guilty verdict was delivered Owen asked that his coffin be brought to the prison for him to inspect but when he suggested that he'd like to sleep in it, the authorities refused. The 8th of August was set as the day of execution.

The night before he made a statement that he was innocent. On the morning of the hanging he again repeated his cry of innocence before tucking into a hearty breakfast. As John Owen stood, the rope around his neck, the white cap over his face, he asked to make a statement. He turned to face the assembled throng and addressed them through the white cloth, "My friends, I am going to die for the murder of Charles - what's his name? I forget, oh! Charles Marshall, but I am innocent!" He then turned around, had his feet tied together, and fell to his death.

The following morning *The Times* reported that, "the circumstances of this horrible tragedy are still fresh in the public recollection, and these, together with other incidents of the prisoner's career, prove him to have been an extraordinary criminal."

The body in the trunk

In 1927 London's Charing Cross Station hit the headlines when the dismembered remains of a female body were discovered inside a trunk deposited at the Left Luggage office. Police soon traced the item to a young estate agent, John Robinson. He had met the victim, Minnie Bonati, at Victoria Station and had taken her to a flat where they had had sex. He then murdered her and took her remains to Charing Cross. At the trial Robinson tried to claim that during a row Minnie had died accidentally - though how she had cut herself up he was unable to explain and the jury found him guilty!

Top: Charing Cross Left Luggage Office
Bottom: Charing Cross Station early in the 20th century

The World of Crime

The kidnapping of a heir

The young dashing Charles Lindbergh entered the record books in 1927 as the first man to travel from New York to Paris in a machine heavier than air. Lindbergh was a major star of his day but he is also remembered for the kidnapping of his son, in 1932.

Little Charlie Lindbergh (left) was found dead after the family had paid a hefty ransom demand. A German, Bruno Hauptmann, was convicted and put to death for the murder despite protesting his innocence. Years later the spotlight fell on Charles Lindbergh himself and there are many who believe he accidentally killed his son and then framed Hauptmann.

Top Right:
Flying ace Charles Lindbergh pictured in 1927

Top Left:
Baby Charlie Lindbergh

Right:
Bruno Hauptmann (centre) who was convicted and executed for the baby's murder

The World of Crime

THOMAS NEILL CREAM
The south London poisoner

IT was the evening of October 13th, 1891, when a man named James Styles watched a young woman topple forward into a brick wall then fall onto the pavement in Waterloo Road, London, as if she were drunk. But Styles, who had watched the girl moments earlier walking in a jaunty manner knew that it wasn't drink which was affecting her, and he ran across to help.

Pulling the girl, later named as nineteen-year-old Ellen Donworth, to her feet, Styles found she was twitching uncontrollably and appeared to be having a fit. Somehow, half carrying her and half dragging her, he struggled until he managed to reach her lodgings in Duke Street, (now Duchy Street) off Westminster Bridge Road, within a stone's throw of the Houses of Parliament.

Joined by several other people who had to hold her down, for such were her convulsions, Ellen was soon screaming in agony and struggling to get loose, at the same time gasping..."A tall gentleman with cross eyes... silk hat... whisk-

Ellen Donworth Pitches forward

ers...gave me drink out of a bottle...white stuff in it." Ellen died before she reached St Thomas' Hospital and Dr. Kelloch could find no immediate reason for her death, but a post-mortem examination of her stomach contents soon revealed the deadly answer; she had been given a dose of strychnine.

The inquest of Ellen Donworth opened four days later, and the Coroner, Mr. GP Wyatt received a letter which read: *I am writing to say that if you and your satellites fail to bring the murderer of Ellen Donworth, alias Ellen Linnell, late of 8, Duke Street, Westminster Bridge Road, to justice, that I am willing to give you such assistance as will bring the murderer to justice, provided your government is willing to pay me £300,000 for my services. No pay if not successful.*

A. O'BRIEN, DETECTIVE

The demand was absurd but typical of many arrogant, over-confident criminals, and it wasn't long before London, which had only just become used to normal life after the notorious Jack the Ripper killings of three years before, was reeling at the audacity of yet another mass killer who in a small area bounded by Blackfriars Road, Lambeth Road and the River Thames, over the next few months was to kill another three women. Like Donworth, they were all prostitutes, and it is perhaps true

Westminster Bridge and St Thomas' Hospital in the early 20th century

to say that the crimes of Thomas Neill Cream were worse than the Ripper murders because Cream left his helpless victims to die a slow agonising death rather than, presumably at least, the swiftness of Jack's knife!

Cream was born in Glasgow on May 27th, 1850, and when he was about three years of age his family decided to emigrate to Canada and his father became manager of a Quebec shipbuilding company. When Thomas was old enough his father found him a job as an apprentice but he found it beneath him, for he was already adopting the pose of a 'dandy' and he asked his father to send him to medical school instead to train to become a doctor. His obviously devoted father agreed, and Cream started studying at M'Gill College in Montreal and was given a generous allowance by his father which he wasted no time in splashing out freely on jewels and even keeping a carriage and pair. During his college years he was known by fellow students, as a ladies-man, and he evidently had little trouble attracting women. He was, however, also a clever student and he was even a Sunday School teacher at one time, and when he graduated as a Medical Doctor on March 31st, 1876, the future seemed very bright indeed for him.

Just after his graduation Cream met Eliza Brooks, the daughter of a hotel owner from Waterloo, about seventy miles from Montreal, and the pair quickly formed a liaison, but only a couple of months later she became very ill and her family doctor claimed she was pregnant but an attempt had been made at an abortion. Eliza's angry father travelled to Montreal and told Cream in no uncertain terms that he had the choice of marrying his daughter at once or getting shot! The choice was not a difficult one, and Cream and Eliza were quickly wed.

Less than twenty-four hours later Cream announced to his new bride that he had to travel to England to finish his medical training. It was the last time the pair saw each other, and less than a year later Eliza died of tuberculosis. Even then Cream showed his totally ruthless spirit by writing to her father saying that under his marriage contract Mr. Brooks owed him $1,000 but he was willing to compromise and accept $200!

Cream had arrived in London in October, 1876, and started studying at St Thomas' Hospital before moving to Edinburgh where he qualified as a surgeon. Just four weeks afterwards he returned to London, Ontario, where he set up in practice, and it was here that he first came to public notice after a chambermaid was found dead behind his surgery and an inquest heard that she had visited Cream to procure an abortion. The inquest also heard that the girl had died "from chloroform administered by some person unknown." Needless to say that with the finger of suspicion pointing in his direction, Cream decided the wisest course was to move on, and he crossed the American frontier into the United States.

On August 23rd, 1880, Cream was charged in Chicago with the murder of Julia Faulkner, a Canadian, after performing an illegal operation at the home of a local woman. Despite the authorities in the city suspecting that he carried on a lucrative profession as an illegal abortionist at his surgery in 434 West Madison Avenue, they did not have enough evidence to convict him for the death of Faulkner and he was acquitted. But one small error has often caught the most cunning criminal and Cream's next piece of audacity was almost responsible for him being hanged. Besides his illegal surgery Cream also had another sideline of selling 'quack' medicines to cure epilepsy, and he soon found himself in demand from those seeking help for themselves or loved ones.

It was in the latter category that Cream came into contact with pretty thirty-three-year old Julia Stott, whose invalid husband Daniel, aged sixty-one, had seen his advertisement in a newspaper in Grand Praire, Boone County, Illinois, and decided to send her to Chicago to buy some medicine. It was a decision that was to change both Julia's and Cream's lives, and one which was to cause Daniel to lose his. There appeared to have been an immediate attraction between Cream and Mrs Stott and she soon became his mistress, visiting the surgery at regular intervals to buy medicine and see her lover. Cream, meanwhile, had tried to insure Daniel Stott's life but had failed, so he decided to do what he was evidently best at – committing murder. Once more he gave Julia Stott medicine for her husband, but this particular prescription contained something more potent than his quack medicine, and within twenty minutes of taking it, on July 14th, 1881, Daniel died in agony, seemingly of a seizure caused by his epilepsy.

For most people that would have been enough, but Cream tried to detract suspicion by being over enthusiastic in his evidence to the authorities that the pharmacist had mistakenly put too much strychnine in Stott's prescription, and he demanded that the coroner order the body to be exhumed. To back up his demand, Cream had persuaded his mistress to hand him power of attorney. At first the coroner thought the letter was the work of a crank and dismissed it, but Cream pursued his crazy scheme and next wrote to the district attorney who ordered an exhumation. The autopsy, which followed, found excessive strychnine in Daniel Stott's body and it didn't take long for the lovers to be arrested and charged with murder. Cream had made a fatal error.

Julia Stott decided to turn state's evidence and thus escaped jail after being acquitted of her husband's murder, but Cream was found guilty of second degree murder and was sentenced to life imprisonment in Illinois's state penitentiary at Joliet. Again luck was on Cream's side, and instead of growing old in Joliet he was released on July 31st, 1891, after serving just ten years of his sentence. His father had died while Cream was in jail and had left him $16,000, so taking his money and doffing his hat to America the killer once again crossed the Atlantic Ocean to England, arriving in Liverpool on October 1st, and turning up in London four days later where he took a room at Anderton's Hotel in Fleet Street for two nights before finding lodgings at 103 Lambeth Palace Road in the heart of the slums of south London.

The day after his arrival in London Cream had made the acquaintance of a prostitute, Elizabeth Masters, in Ludgate Circus and taken her to a public house for a drink before taking her back to her rooms just off Lambeth Road and afterwards to Gatti's Music Hall in Westminster Bridge Road. In Gatti's bar the pair were joined by a girl called Elizabeth May who lodged in the room next to Masters, and after several more drinks they went to a public house in Ludgate Circus. Cream told Masters that he would write to her to arrange another meeting.

Westminster Bridge Road as it looks today

Masters later wrote: "He said that in his younger days he was a student at St Thomas' Hospital. He showed me a photograph of his mother and one of himself. He said he was staying at a hotel in Fleet Street. While he showed me the photographs he took off his hat. I think he had glasses on at the time. I noticed a peculiar look in his eyes and that he had a squint."

Shortly after taking up lodgings in Lambeth Palace Road, Cream was advertising himself as Dr. Thomas Neill, MD. and he was making himself known at a local pharmacy at 22 Parliament Street where he told the assistant that he was studying at St Thomas' Hospital and asked for a quantity of nux vomica which contains strychnine. It was a quantity of this poison, which was later given to Ellen Donworth who had known Cream simply as "Fred".

Houses in Lambeth Road, identical to those known by Cream

Three days after their first meeting, Elizabeth Masters received a note from Cream saying he would call between three and five o' clock that afternoon, Friday, October 9th, and asked her not to destroy the letter until he called! Elizabeth showed the note to a friend, Elizabeth May, and they both spent the afternoon gazing out of the window of their lodgings looking out for him. They suddenly spotted Cream coming along the street following another woman named Matilda Clover, who kept turning to give him smiles of encouragement. The two Elizabeth's put on their hats and decided to follow them and they saw Clover stop outside her lodging house at 27 Lambeth Road until she was joined by Cream, and the pair then went inside together.

Eleven days later a servant named Lucy Rose was cleaning Matilda Clover's room when she came across a note lying open on the table and curiosity caused her to read it. It said: "Meet me outside the Canterbury at 7.30 if you can come clean and sober. Do you remember the night I bought you your boots? You were so drunk that you could not speak to me. Please bring this paper and envelope with you." It was signed "Fred".

Later that night Lucy opened the door and found Matilda Clover and her escort waiting to come in. Lucy later told the court at Cream's trial: "There was the light of a small paraffin lamp in the hall. The gentleman was tall and broad and had a heavy moustache...I should say he was about forty. He was wearing a large coat with a cape to it, and a high silk hat. I had never seen him before...After that the gentleman went out; Clover did not go out; she bade the man goodnight at the door. I heard her say 'goodnight, dear,' as she let him out...

"After going to bed, I went to sleep. I was awoke about three o'clock by loud screams. I slept in the back room, under where Clover slept. I called the landlady and went into Clover's room and found her lying across the foot of the bed with her head fixed between the bedstead and the wall. She told me she had been poisoned by pills given her by the gentleman.

"She was apparently in great agony. During her agony she screamed as if in great pain. There were moments when she appeared to have relief, and then the fit came on again. When the fits were upon her she was all of a twitch. She said once she thought she was going to die, and she said she would like to see her baby.

"When the fit of agony was on her, her eyes rolled about terribly...She died at a quarter to nine the same morning. In her moments of relief she was quite calm and collected. It was in one of those moments of relief that she made the statement about dying and her desire to see the child. The landlady went for medical help. Mr. Coppin, assistant to Dr. M'Carthy, came, I think, about seven. Clover had been drinking the previous night. I noticed it.

"Mr. Coppin sent for some medicine. The first drop I gave her she turned black. We sent Mrs. Phillips' grandson for it. As she got worse, Mrs Phillips went again for Mr. Coppin but he did not come. Clover was getting worse. During that early morning she vomited a good deal. Dr. Graham came for the first time in the middle of the day; he gave the certificate of death. He had not seen her that morning, not until she was dead. She was buried at Tooting on October 27th, by the parish."

At first impression it might appear shocking that the doctor, Coppin, would not pay a second visit to the dying woman, but Clover was a heavy drinker and had been receiving treatment for alcoholic poisoning by Dr. Graham, and it was assumed by both men that Clover was suffering with delirium tremens (DT's), and her death certificate gave the cause of death as "primarily delirium tremens, secondly syncope."

Both Ellen Donworth and Matilda Clover had died within a week of each other from acute poisoning which should have been enough to have stirred suspicion among medical men of the time, but it seems that nobody was aware of any connection, or, indeed, of the correct causes of death, and Cream was able to carry our his evil work with impunity. He may also have been able to continue his crimes for a long time except for the biggest folly of his character – his capacity for self-publicity!

Several days after Clover's death Cream met and wooed a woman named Lou Harris from St John's Wood where she lived with a painter. The pair quickly became intimate in a local hotel and Cream told her the following morning that she had spots on her forehead and said he would arrange to get her some pills to remove them if she would meet him the following evening at the Embankment.

At the time suggested, Harris, accompanied by a friend who stood some way off, met Cream who handed her two pills from his waistcoat pocket. He told her to take them there and then, but to swallow them and not to bite into them. Harris later said: "He put them into my right hand. I pretended to take them, putting my hand to my mouth and pretending to swallow them, but I passed them into my left hand. He asked me to show him my right hand; I showed it to him, it was empty; then he asked me to show him my left hand in which I had the pills. I threw the pills away behind me and showed him my left hand."

Cream then suggested to Harris that he call her a cab, making an excuse that he was needed at St Thomas' Hospital but promised he would join her at eleven o'clock that night. Although Harris turned up, needless to say Cream did not.

A month later he sent a letter signed "M. Malone" and dated November 28th, to Dr. William Henry Broadbent, which read:

*"Sir,
Miss Clover, who, until a short time ago, lived at 27 Lambeth Road S., died at the above address on October 20 (last month) through being poisoned with strychnine. After her death a search of her effects was made, and evidence was found which showed that you not only gave her the medicine which caused her death, but that you had been hired for the purpose of poisoning her. The evidence is in the hands of one of our detectives, who will give the evidence either to you or to the police authorities for the sum of £2,500 sterling..."*

The following month Countess Russell, staying at the Savoy Hotel in London, also received a letter accusing her husband, Lord Russell, of the murder of Clover. It was a singular series of letters which can either be put down as sheer stupidity by Cream, as the work of an obvious madman, or total arrogance on his behalf, perhaps believing that despite taunting the police and others he was still incapable of being captured.

Savoy Hotel

Whatever else he was, he was certainly restless and he decided to cross the Atlantic once again, leaving for America in January 1892 and returning two months later to his lodgings at 103 Lambeth Palace Road on April 9th. Three days later police constable George Cumley was on his beat at 1.45am when he saw a man leaving 118 Stamford Street and saying goodnight to a woman. The PC described the man as about fifty-years old, with a moustache, dark overcoat and tall, silk hat, and wearing glasses. The house, he said later, was occupied by two prostitutes, Alice Marsh, aged twenty-one, and Emma Shrivell, aged eighteen, each paying seven shillings and sixpence rent for their rooms on the second floor.

Forty-five minutes later the house was filled with agonising shrieks which woke the landlady who hurried to the passageway of the house where she found Alice Marsh in agony on the floor. She sent for a hansom cab and a constable and was suddenly shocked to hear a cry from upstairs. Leaving Alice in the passageway the landlady rushed to Emma Shrivell's room and found her also on the floor in agony. Torn between the two women on different floors, each writhing uncontrollably, it was a relief when her husband returned with PC Eversfield, who gave each girl mustard and water in an attempt to make them empty their stomach of the poison. But it was in vain, and Alice died on the way to hospital, while Emma hung on in great pain for a further six hours.

Between convulsions, Emma had spoken to PC Cumley and she told him that a man called "Fred", claiming he was a doctor, had given each of the girls three long pills following a meal of tinned salmon and bottled beer. She described him and Cumley confirmed with her that it was the same man he had seen leaving the house earlier.

There now followed the same pattern as before, with Cream writing a letter to Dr. Joseph Harper, the father of medical student W.J. Harper, one of his fellow lodgers at 103 Lambeth Palace Road, in which he claimed that his son had committed the murders of Alice Marsh and Emma Shrivell. The letter also contained the information that for £1,500 pounds the "evidence" of the murders would be "suppressed." Strangely, these attempts at blackmail were never taken any further by Cream, and criminal experts have since explained that this was undoubtedly proof that he was insane.

Left:

Ludgate Circus, London, where Thomas Cream met Elizabeth Masters and Elizabeth May, both of whom later followed him to 27 Lambeth Road

Time was running out on Cream's extraordinary run of luck, however, and after he again called attention to himself by repeating his accusation against young Harper in a letter to the foreman of the jury at the inquest of Marsh and Shrivell, an order was granted by the Home Office for Scotland Yard to exhume the body of Matilda Clover, and detectives now started to shadow Cream and watch his lodgings. Even when an acquaintance, John Haynes, pointed out to Cream that police were watching him, his arrogance refused to believe it, and he told Haynes that they were watching Harper who lived in the same house.

Detective Inspector Tunbridge had been ordered to look into the poisoning mysteries in south Lambeth, and he visited Cream on May 26th at his rooms where the killer complained about police officers following him. He also showed the inspector a leather case containing a bottle of strychnine pills and other drugs that he said were only sold to doctors and chemists.

The next step by Tunbridge was to visit Dr. Joseph Harper in Barnstaple where he was shown the threatening letter accusing his son of the murders of Marsh and Shrivell, which had been written in Cream's handwriting, which was recognised at once by the inspector who suggested to Dr. Harper that Cream should be arrested and charged with attempted blackmail. Tunbridge caught up with Cream and arrested him on June 3rd, as he was planning to make his getaway across the Atlantic once more.

Cream was charged at Bow Street Magistrates Court the following day with attempting to extort money from Dr. Joseph Harpcr, and the case was adjourned until June 28th, which gave detectives the time they needed to chase further clues which, Tunbridge was now convinced, would see Cream hanged for murder.

Matilda Clover's body had been exhumed on May 5th, 1892, and examined by Dr. Thomas Stevenson, who gave evidence to the inquest, which began almost seven weeks later. It lasted just three days and the verdict read "that Matilda Clover died of strychnine poisoning, and that the poison was administered by Thomas Neill with intent to destroy life. We therefore find him guilty of wilful murder."

It was a singular verdict from a coroner's jury, but it was enough to see Cream appear before Mr. Justice Hawkins at the Central Criminal Court on October 17th, 1892, charged with murder. It was the third time in his life that he had faced the might of the law, but it was definitely a case of third time unlucky for Cream despite reports that he gave his usual performance of bravado and insolence in the court. Contemporary reports even state that he was so confident at escaping the gallows once again that he actually danced and sang in his cell. But his fate was sealed, and the jury returned a unanimous verdict of "guilty" to the murder charge.

This time Cream fell silent while Mr. Justice Hawkins donned the traditional black cap of a British court and sentenced him to death, but as he was being taken from the court he said: "They shall never hang me!"

This time, however, there was no escape, and on the morning of November 15th, 1892, Thomas Neill Cream was hanged in Newgate Prison. It has been reported that as he stood on the trap door of the gallows with the hood over his head and the noose around his neck, he shouted the words "I am Jack..." just as the trap was sprung. Many have believed that this was a last minute confession that he was Jack the Ripper, but it is more likely to have been another last minute spark of inspiration by Cream which he hoped would have stopped the execution from going ahead by the mere intrigue of his comment, but he was too late, and Cream died a far less painful death than his poor hapless victims.

The Central Criminal Court, better known as The Old Bailey, from where Cream was senteced to death

THE FLYPAPER POISONER
The case of Frederick Seddon

IN his autobiography *'Diary of a Hangman'*, John Ellis, the official executioner from 1901 – 1924 reveals that he rarely ever attended a court case. He visited the Old Bailey just once - to hear the first day of the murder case of Frederick Seddon and his wife in March 1912. Ellis's account paints a vivid picture of a hard man obsessed with money.

Born in Liverpool the young Seddon took to the sea only to find himself shipwrecked off Cape Horn. He was eventually rescued and given passage to the Falkland Islands where he acquired some land and became a sheep farmer. After some time he returned to Liverpool and again found work as a mariner. By the time he reached his late teens he had seen much of the world. He then decided that he wanted some time ashore and found a job with an insurance company collecting and selling policies. Seddon did well and was much respected by his employers, so much so that they moved him to Islington in London and promoted him.

Frederick Seddon, his wife and their five children moved into 63 Tollington Park in the Finsbury Park district of the capital. They decided to take in a lodger and chose one who would turn out to be very cantankerous indeed. Eliza Mary Barrow was a spinster in her late forties who was thought by those who knew her to be eccentric. Whether Seddon knew it at this stage or not – she was also very wealthy. Barrow had £1,600 invested in India stocks, kept a quantity of gold under her bed and owned a substantial amount of London property each bringing in regular rents. Due to her often erratic behaviour her family had all but deserted her and so Barrow began to rely on Seddon's financial advice. The result of this trusting relationship was that the spinster signed everything over to him in return for an annual annuity of £72. It wasn't actually a bad deal and over the rest of her life she would be well cared for. Seddon though, had other plans.

In the summer of 1911 Eliza Barrow fell ill and was suffering from what was described in court as "epidemic diarrhoea". Within two weeks she was dead. The Seddons had nursed her themselves, no doctor had ever been troubled. Around the room hung fly papers to keep her as comfortable as possible in her final hours. Another week on and Eliza's relations heard the dreadful news of her death and so they paid a visit to Tollington Park. They were shocked to say the least when Seddon informed them that he was most surprised that they hadn't replied to his letter informing them of Eliza's death and inviting them to the funeral. Yes, Eliza Barrow had already been buried. One of the relatives enquired how Seddon had gained access to the family vault and they were shocked even further when he informed them that the wealthy deceased had been given a pauper's burial. It was later discovered that Seddon had even haggled with the undertaker and got the pauper's price down from £4 to £3. 7s. 6d. The family demanded she be exhumed and reburied with her parents.

The police were called in and discovered that just days before her death Barrow had signed a will making Seddon executor and trustee to her estate. This, combined with the obvious benefits if he were no longer required to pay her the annual annuity, provided a motive for murder. When her body was exhumed it was found to contain large quantities of arsenic. Mr and Mrs Seddon were charged with murder.

The couple claimed that they had always had a very caring relationship with Barrow – far better, it was pointed, out than her own family. They had nursed her through her illness, hadn't called a doctor because there didn't seem a need, and once she had died had searched her room for cash. Finding just £10 they had used that to bury her. Mrs Seddon informed the court that they had sent flowers – at their own expense. But how had the arsenic been administered? At that time fly papers were made from arsenic and it was alleged that these had been soaked in water to loosen the poison which had then been given to the old lady. Gradually it became clear that the prosecution would allow Mrs Seddon to escape justice if her husband could be hung. The jury did what was asked of them – Frederick Seddon was found guilty, his wife, not guilty. Then events took a dramatic turn. Seddon asked for permission to address the judge, Justice Bucknill, prior to sentencing. This was allowed.

"The prosecution have not traced anything to me in the shape of money, which is the great motive suggested by the prosecution for me to commit this diabolical crime, of which I declare before the Great Architect of the Universe I am not guilty."

Seddon in the Dock of the Old Bailey

This was a coded reference to fellow masons in the court that Seddon was a member of his local lodge. Masons can do nothing greater than to swear unto the 'Great Architect' and fellow masons are obliged to accept this oath. Justice Bucknill was Provincial Grand Master of the Surrey Lodge and the accused obviously knew this. His private beliefs were about to clash with his duty. With tears rolling down his cheeks he looked Seddon firmly in the eye, "Both you and I belong to the same brotherhood and that makes it doubly painful for me, although it makes no difference to my duty." With that he sentenced him to hang on 18th April 1912 at Pentonville.

Mrs Seddon campaigned for a reprieve right up to the last minute but to no avail and he was indeed executed. There is just one footnote to this case – Frederick Seddon denied that he was obsessed with money however, just days before he died his lawyers visited him in prison to tell him how much some of his effects had raised at auction. He was furious that the sum was so little and slammed his fists on the table crying, "That's done it!". If Seddon had not come over to the jury as a cold killer there's some doubt whether he would have been executed at all – the evidence wasn't really strong enough.

THE GIRL ON THE SWING
Harry Kendall Thaw

EVELYN Nesbit was beautiful, ambitious and keen to taste the finer things in life. After completing her education she used her looks to gain work as an artist's model before landing a plum job in the chorus line of a production of the musical "Floradora". She was still only fifteen.

It was whilst performing in the show that she met wealthy socialite and architect Stanford White. White, who designed Madison Square Garden, invited Evelyn and one of her friends back to his luxury apartment where he famously had a red velvet swing which the girls would sit on as he pushed them - often for hours! White began to see Evelyn on a regular basis, she often posed for exotic photographs, played on his swing and eventually - at the age of sixteen, became his mistress. Oh yes, White was married.

This fact didn't stop Stanford showing his young girlfriend off however, and they became famous on New York's socialite circle. It was around this time that Evelyn was introduced to Harry K. Thaw, the handsome son of a Pittsburgh railway magnate. Slowly their friendship developed and they hatched a plan - she would run off with Harry and they would marry but in order to escape White once and for all, they would have to leave the country.

And that is exactly what happened - the young couple, Evelyn was still not yet twenty, eloped to the pretty Tyrolean castle at Schloss Katzenstein where they planned to wed. But Evelyn had not bargained on a new revelation - Harry had a nasty side to him. On their first morning, he stripped her naked at breakfast, produced a bullwhip, and he whipped and beat her so hard that she was in bed for three weeks suffering from his actions. Why she went ahead with the marriage we will probably never know but here was a girl who knew White would never marry her, who had turned her back on her life and friends in New York and who must have been seduced by Thaw's tremendous wealth. For whatever reason or reasons, Evelyn became Mrs Thaw on 4th April 1905 having journeyed back to America for the big society affair.

Harry's family took the young couple in and against their better judgement decided to make the best of a bad lot. Evelyn then discovered that many of Harry's ex lovers had suffered in the way she had and some had even survived being strangled by him. As time went on so Harry Thaw lost his grip - he purchased a pistol and began to take an unhealthy interest in guns and duelling. On 25th June 1906 they went to New York where Harry treated his bride to a special dinner at Cafe Martin before joining friends at Madison Square Garden for a performance of the revue "Mam 'zelle Champagne". Shortly after they took their table, White arrived and took a nearby seat. The Thaw party were not enjoying what was a dull production and at the interval Evelyn suggested they leave and go on somewhere else. As she reached the foyer she turned to notice her husband had abandoned her.

"I saw him sitting there, big, fat and healthy," Thaw later told the District Attorney, "and there Evelyn was, poor delicate little thing, all trembling and nervous." In seconds, White was on the floor, dying, covered in blood. The room erupted with screams everywhere. Harry Thaw, still and controlled, stood with the smoking gun in his hand. The irony of course, was that Stanford White was to die in the very concert hall that he had designed, that was the crowning glory of his career. "I am glad I killed him, he ruined my wife," Thaw was to tell the crowd.

Stanford White

Thaw then turned and joined his wife and friends and he was eventually disarmed in an elevator. The powerful and wealthy Thaw family swung into action - not to defend the actions of their own flesh and blood but to poison White's reputation. It was a battle no one could win - both men were as black in character as the other.

In January 1907 the trial began and after four months of testimony the jury was split -seven found Thaw guilty and five not guilty on grounds of insanity. A second trial was set for the following year and Thaw's lawyers decided to try for the insanity loophole. Evidence of madness within the Thaw family was presented, a brothel keeper testified that Harry had beaten her regularly and so on ... such that a unanimous verdict was brought in - Harry Thaw was not guilty by reason of insanity.

Thaw was sent to the New York State Asylum for the Criminally Insane. His family, always with one eye on the press, pushed for him to be released but it was not to be. However, in 1913 he escaped, climbing in to the back of a waiting car and making across the border to Canada. His freedom lasted just one month and after a great deal of diplomatic pressure being exerted by the American government he was sent back over the border and taken to a jail in New Hampshire. A few months later and he was back in New York where he remained until July 1915. His family never stopped campaigning for his release - and eventually, their efforts paid off. At a third trial not only was he found to be sane but the jury also decided that he was innocent of all charges.

With Harry out of the asylum, Evelyn filed for divorce and moved away to start her life again - this time out of the limelight. Harry though, fared a little worse. He had a row with a young lad in Kansas City and, reacting in his usual fashion, kidnapped and whipped the poor lad. He was arrested, found guilty, declared insane and taken to an asylum. In 1924 however, following the previous pattern, he was re-trialed, found to be innocent, found to be sane and released. He went to live in Florida where he died of a coronary in 1947, the peaceful end to a most extraordinary story. In recent years, the tale has been brushed off and woven into the storyline of the smash-hit musical "Ragtime". Evelyn's character sings a haunting solo - "The Girl On The Swing!"